Conflict and Diplomacy in the Middle East

External Actors and Regional Rivalries

EDITED BY
YANNIS A. STIVACHTIS

E-INTERNATIONAL
RELATIONS
PUBLISHING

E-International Relations
www.E-IR.info
Bristol, England
2018

ISBN 978-1-910814-49-9

This book is published under a Creative Commons CC BY-NC 4.0 license. You are free to:

- **Share** — copy and redistribute the material in any medium or format
- **Adapt** — remix, transform, and build upon the material

Under the following terms:

- **Attribution** — You must give appropriate credit, provide a link to the license, and indicate if changes were made. You may do so in any reasonable manner, but not in any way that suggests the licensor endorses you or your use.
- **NonCommercial** — You may not use the material for commercial purposes.

Any of the above conditions can be waived if you get permission. Please contact info@e-ir.info for any such enquiries, including for licensing and translation requests.
Other than the terms noted above, there are no restrictions placed on the use and dissemination of this book for student learning materials/scholarly use.

Production: Michael Tang
Cover Image: Meysam Azarneshin

A catalogue record for this book is available from the British Library.

E-IR Edited Collections

Series Editors: Stephen McGlinchey, Marianna Karakoulaki & Agnieszka Pikulicka-Wilczewska
Books Editor: Cameran Clayton
Editorial assistance: Jane Kirkpatrick, Corey McCabe, Adeleke Olumide Ogunnoiki and Andrei Sterescu

E-IR's Edited Collections are open access scholarly books presented in a format that preferences brevity and accessibility while retaining academic conventions. Each book is available in print and digital versions and is published under a Creative Commons license. As E-International Relations is committed to open access in the fullest sense, free electronic versions of all of our books, including this one, are available on our website.

Find out more at: http://www.e-ir.info/publications

About the E-International Relations website

E-International Relations (www.E-IR.info) is the world's leading open access website for students and scholars of international politics, reaching over 3 million readers annually. E-IR's daily publications feature expert articles, blogs, reviews and interviews – as well as student learning resources. The website is run by a registered non-profit organisation based in Bristol, UK and staffed with an all-volunteer team of students and scholars.

Abstract

The Middle East's geographical and strategic uniqueness has made every great power in history to seek to advance its interests in the region. Yet, the region constitutes the greatest single reserve of oil in the world, which has made it a regular source of foreign interference in the post-World War II era. In addition to its geographical and strategic uniqueness, the Middle East is the birthplace and spiritual center of the three most important monotheistic religions, namely Christianity, Judaism and Islam. Due to its geopolitical importance, any inter- and intra-state conflict in the Middle East has the potential not only for destabilizing the region as a whole or upsetting the regional balance of power but also affecting global stability. For these reasons, the Middle East has been a major center of world affairs; an economically, politically, and culturally sensitive area.

This volume provides an account of international relations in the contemporary Middle East. After employing the Regional Security Complex Theory (RSCT) in order to define and delimit the region of the Middle East, individual chapters are dedicated to addressing the question of regional order, examining how regionalism and globalism feature in Middle Eastern integration processes, exploring regional bids for hegemony, and investigating the approaches and policies of major international actors, such as the United States, Russia, China, the European Union and the United Nations.

Editor

Yannis A. Stivachtis is an Associate Professor of Political Science at Virginia Polytechnic Institute & State University, USA.

Contributors

Jonathan Cristol is a Research Fellow at the Levermore Global Scholars Program, Adelphi University (NY) and Senior Fellow at the Center for Civic Engagement, Bard College (NY), USA.

Xi Chen is an Associate Professor of Political Science at the University of Texas Rio Grande Valley, USA.

Ali G. Dizboni is an Associate Professor at the Department of Political Science, Royal Military College of Canada (RMCC).

Onur Erpul is a Fulbright Scholar and PhD candidate in International Relations at Florida International University, USA.

Stefanie Georgakis Abbott is Assistant Director of Presidential Studies at the Miller Center, University of Virginia, USA.

Spyridon N. Litsas is an Associate Professor of International Relations at the University of Macedonia, Thessaloniki, Greece.

Allison Miller is a PhD Candidate in Globalization and Governance at the School for Public and International Affairs (SPIA), Virginia Polytechnic Institute & State University, USA.

Sofwat Omar is a Research Fellow at the Department of Political Science, Royal Military College of Canada (RMCC).

Ayşegül Sever is a Professor of International Relations at Marmara University, Istanbul, Turkey.

Contents

INTRODUCTION
    Yannis A. Stivachtis   1

1. GLOBALISM, REGIONALISM AND THE MIDDLE EAST
    Ayşegül Sever   16

2. THE CHALLENGES TO MIDDLE EASTERN INTERNATIONAL SOCIETY: A STUDY IN DISORDER
    Onur Erpul   32

3. UNITED STATES FOREIGN POLICY IN THE MIDDLE EAST AFTER THE COLD WAR
    Jonathan Cristol   48

4. RUSSIAN FOREIGN POLICY IN THE MIDDLE EAST UNDER PUTIN: CAN BEARS WALK IN THE DESERT?
    Spyridon N. Litsas   64

5. CHINA IN THE POST-HEGEMONIC MIDDLE EAST: A WARY DRAGON?
    Xi Chen   78

6. THE EU AND THE MIDDLE EAST: FROM THE EURO-MEDITERRANEAN PARTNERSHIP TO THE UNION FOR THE MEDITERRANEAN
    Stefanie Georgakis Abbott   93

7. THE EU AND THE MIDDLE EAST: THE EUROPEAN NEIGHBORHOOD POLICY (ENP)
    Yannis A. Stivachtis   110

8. THE UNITED NATIONS AND MIDDLE EASTERN SECURITY
    Allison Miller   128

9. HEGEMONIC ASPIRATIONS AND MIDDLE EAST DISCORD: THE CASE OF IRAN
    Ali G. Dizboni & Sofwat Omar   144

NOTE ON INDEXING   166

Introduction

YANNIS A. STIVACHTIS

The Middle East occupies a unique geographical and strategic position. Hence, it is not a coincidence that every great power in history has sought to advance its interests in the region. In addition to its geographical and strategic uniqueness, the Middle East is the birthplace and spiritual center of the three most important monotheistic religions, namely Christianity, Judaism and Islam, as well as the greatest single reserve of oil. Last, but not least, due to its geopolitical importance, any inter- and intra-state conflict in the Middle East has the potential not only of destabilizing the region as a whole or upsetting the regional balance of power but also affecting global stability. For these reasons, the Middle East has been a major center of world affairs; an economically, politically, and culturally sensitive area. The purpose of this volume is to provide an account of international relations in the contemporary Middle East. To address the question of regional order, attention will focus on the policies of external actors – such as the United States (US), Russia, China, the European Union, and the United Nations – as well as on regional hegemonic aspirations and resulting rivalries.

Defining and Delimiting the Middle East as a Region

No unanimity exists on a definition of the Middle East – even the name of the region has not been universally accepted. For the purpose of this volume, the definition of the Middle East region will be based on Barry Buzan's Regional Security Complex Theory (RSCT) that was introduced in the first edition of *People, States and Fear* (1983, 105–15). RSCT provides a theoretical justification for constructing world regions based on the degree of enmity and amity existing among states. Updates to the theory were presented in Buzan (1991, chapter 5 and 2016, chapter 5), while a revised version of RSCT was presented by Barry Buzan, Ole Wæver and Jaap de Wilde in 1998 and by Buzan and Wæver in 2003.

Regional Security Complex Theory (RSCT)

A more traditional way to define a region is with reference to the balance of power theory. However, to define a region, the principal element that Buzan has added to power relations among states is the pattern of amity and enmity existing among them (Buzan 1991, 189). 'Amity' refers to inter-state relationships ranging from genuine friendship to expectation of protection or support. 'Enmity', on the other hand, refers to inter-state relationships conditioned by suspicion and fear.

The balance of power theory would consider the patterns of amity and enmity as a product of the balance of power, with states shifting their alignments in accordance with the dictates of movements in the distribution of power. However, Buzan has correctly pointed out that the historical dynamic of amity and enmity is only partly related to the balance of power, and that where it is related, it is much more durable than the relatively fluid movement of the distribution of power (Buzan 1991, 190). Moreover, patterns of amity and enmity arise from a variety of issues ranging from border disputes and ideological alignments to longstanding historical links – whether positive or negative – and which could not be predicted from a simple consideration of the distribution of power (Buzan 1991, 190). Enmity can be particularly durable when it acquires a historical character between peoples, as it has between the Arabs and the Israelis or the Iranians and the Iraqis. Consequently, the two patterns, namely power relations and enmity/amity, should be considered as distinct factors.

Patterns of amity and enmity among states can, therefore, be used to define a region by focusing on their security relations. The term 'security complex' is used by Buzan to label the resulting formations. A security complex is defined as "a group of states whose primary security concerns link together sufficiently closely that their national securities cannot realistically be considered apart from one another" (Buzan 1991, 190). Thus, the term 'security complex' indicates both the character of the attribute that defines the set (security), and the notion of intense interdependence that distinguishes any particular set from its neighbors. Security complexes emphasize the interdependence of rivalry, as well as that of shared interests.

Working from the perspective of securitization, Barry Buzan, Ole Wæver and Jaap de Wilde have sought to revise Buzan's original definition of security complexes. In doing so, they have still maintained that security interdependence is markedly more intense among the units inside such complexes than with units outside them and that security complexes are about the relative intensities of security relations that lead to distinctive regional patterns shaped both by distribution of power and relations of amity and enmity. The difference is that they have now defined a security complex, as a set of units whose major processes of securitization, desecuritization, or both are so interlinked that their security problems cannot be reasonably analyzed or resolved apart from one another (Buzan, Wæver and de Wilde 1998, 201).

Merging and applying the above two definitions, the Middle East security complex can be defined as a group of states whose primary security concerns, resulting from their processes of securitization, desecuritization, or both are so interlinked that their security problems cannot realistically be considered, analyzed or resolved apart from one another.

The idea of security complexes is an empirical phenomenon with historical and geopolitical roots. Security complexes are also generated by the interaction of anarchy and geography. The political structure of anarchy confronts all states with the power-security dilemma, but security interdependence is powerfully mediated by the effects of geography. Because threats operate more potently over short distances, security interactions with states in close proximity tend to have first priority. However, geographical proximity or even sharing of borders do not necessarily imply the presence of strong security interdependence among states. For example, security interdependence between Iran and Israel is much stronger than Iran's security interdependence with Pakistan, which indicates that Iran and Pakistan belong to different security complexes.

The task of identifying a security complex requires making judgements about the relative strength of patterns of amity and enmity and consequently of security interdependence among different countries. In some places, patterns of amity and enmity are very strong while in others they are relatively weak. In some places the interdependence can be positive, as between Jordan and Egypt – while in others negative, as between Israel and Iran. Usually, security complexes will arise from local relationships, but when outside actors are involved a set of states can be bound together in response to this intrusion. For example, US support for Israel has often brought Arab states together in opposition.

A security complex exists where a set of security relationships stands out by virtue of its relative strong, inward-looking character, and the relative weakness of its outward security interactions with its neighbors (Buzan 1991, 193). In other words, security interdependence will be more strongly focused among the members of the set than they are between the members and outside states. For example, the strong security links between Israel and Syria put these two countries clearly within the same security complex, while the relatively weak links between Iran and Pakistan suggest that these two states belong to two different security complexes.

The principal factor defining a complex is usually a high level of threat and fear, which is felt mutually among two or more states. The Arab–Israeli and the Iranian–Israeli cases clearly show the extent to which neighboring local dynamics are conditioned by the security rhetoric of the states towards each other, by their military deployments, and by the record of their conflicts. On the other hand, the relationship between Egypt and Jordan indicates that a high level of trust and friendship can also serve as a binding force. This is because security interdependence can be positive as well as negative.

Power relations and patterns of amity and enmity among states constitute the basis for assessing whether a regional security complex exists. But are there any additional factors that could serve to define regional security complexes?

Additional Factors Determining the Composition of Regional Security Complexes

Cultural, religious, racial and ethnic ties may also constitute a factor in identifying security complexes since shared cultural characteristics among a group of states would cause them both to pay more attention to each other in general, and to legitimize mutual interventions in each other's security affairs in particular. For example, it is not difficult to see how ethnicity (Arab) and religion (Islam) have facilitated and legitimized security interdependence among a large group of states in the Middle East.

Ethno-cultural thinking underlies much traditional historical analysis. This factor is particularly clear in the Middle East where the idea of an Arab nation, and the trans-national political force of Islam combine to create a potent regional political realm. Arab nationalism and Islam weaken the identity of the local states, legitimize an unusually high degree of security inter-penetration and stimulate a marked propensity to establish regional organizations (the Arab League, the Gulf Cooperation Council, the Arab Cooperation Council, and the Maghreb Group). They also play a major part in defining the main nodes of conflict in the region centered on two non-Arab states embedded within it (Israel and Iran) one of which is not Islamic and the other is the representative of Islam's principal schism. Although cultural, religious, racial and ethnic ties may be important contributing factors in defining the shape and structure of regional security complexes, they nevertheless come second to the patterns of amity and enmity which is the principal defining factor.

Another way in which security complexes can be identified is with reference to the role of economic factors. Usually, in looking for the set of states that constitute security complexes, one is primarily concerned with the military, political and societal dimensions of security. The reason for which these sectors are the most relevant to the patterns of threat and amity/enmity that define the set is because economic relations are not nearly so much conditioned by geographical proximity, as are the military, political and societal ones. Consequently, the problem of economic security is likely to have a quite different relational dynamic from that of military, societal and political security. In most world regions, where local political and military interdependence is strong, economic relations follow a much more wide-ranging pattern that has little to do with the region. Under such conditions, the economic security of regional states does not depend primarily on their relationship with the other states within the same complex.

Economic factors, however, do play a role determining both the power of states within their local security complexes and their domestic stability and cohesion as actors. They may also play an important role in motivating the patterns of external interest in the local complex as in the case of the US and the oil-producing countries of the Persian Gulf. Yet, they can affect the prospects for regional integration, which can influence and determine how a given security complex evolves. Therefore, economic factors need to be taken into account in defining or analyzing a security complex. However, as in the case of the cultural, religious, racial and ethnic ties, economic factors come second to the patterns of amity and enmity which is the principal defining factor.

The Composition and Boundaries of Regional Security Complexes

Buzan (1991, 195) draws a distinction between a 'lower' and a 'higher-level' security complex. A lower level complex is composed of local states whose power does not extend much beyond the range of their immediate neighbors or states with which are in a relatively close proximity. A higher-level security complex, by contrast, includes great powers whose capabilities extend far beyond their immediate environment and whose power is sufficient to impinge on several regions. Consequently, the active involvement of Russia and the US in the Middle East reflects the existence of a high-level security complex.

Security complexes will often include a number of small states. For example, despite their size the small Gulf States are members of the Middle East security complex. Due to their relative low power in comparison with their neighbors, these states may have little impact on the structure of the complex. Moreover, the security of small states is intimately bound up in the pattern of relations among larger states, but they can only become a source of threat to a larger state by virtue of the impact of their alignments on relations among the larger powers. The position of Lebanon in the Middle East security complex is illustrative as the influence of Iran over that country constitutes a central feature of the Iranian–Israeli security relationship.

Another question that has been raised by Buzan is whether regional security complexes are exclusive or overlapping. Although David Lake and Patrick Morgan (1997) have argued that security complexes can have overlapping membership, Buzan and Wæver (2003, 48) have taken the position that regional security complexes are mutually exclusive. Therefore, no single Middle East state can be part of two different security complexes. Instead, Buzan and Wæver have promoted the idea that some states occupy insulating positions between neighboring security complexes. These insulators may exist in relative isolation from the security dynamics on either side, or they may face both ways on the edges of neighboring complexes with or without linking them. Turkey constitutes a clear example as the country separates the Middle East security complex from the European security complex. Likewise, Afghanistan insulates the Middle East Security complex from the South Asia security complex.

Buzan (1991, 198–9) identifies three conditions that explain why it can be difficult to locate the boundaries of security complexes whose existence is not in doubt – such as the Middle East security complex. The first is simply that the boundary between two security complexes is dissolving in a major change in the pattern of regional security dynamics. The second involves the existence of the lopsided security interdependence that occurs when higher and lower level complexes are physically adjacent. However, none of these two conditions is currently present to prevent the identification of the boundaries of the Middle East security complex. Instead, the most relevant condition pertains to a situation in which two or more nodes of security interdependence exist within a group of states, which there are also grounds for thinking of this group as a single security complex.

Specifically, the Middle East contains 25 or so states divided into a number of sub-complexes that have distinct dynamics within the overall Middle East security complex. Buzan and Wæver (2003, 188–193) identify three main sub-complexes which are centered on the Persian Gulf (Iran, Iraq and Saudi Arabia as the principals), the Levant (Israel, Syria and Egypt as the principals), and the Maghreb (with Algeria, Morocco and Libya as the principals). All these nodes have their own distinctive dynamics, but there is enough crossing of boundaries within the Middle Eastern security complex to justify identifying the larger formation as the main regional unit. For example, Syria plays an important role in the Gulf sub-complex by allying with Iran, and Iran plays a crucial role in the Levant supporting Syria and Lebanon against

Israel. Nearly all of the Arab states take some part in the opposition to Israel, which seeks to stir up inter-Arab and inter-Islamic rivalries whenever it can. Yet, the Arab League provides a legitimizing forum in which the affairs of the different sub-complexes are linked together, and which helps to differentiate Middle Eastern security affairs from those of Asia, Europe and Africa.

The Structure of Regional Security Complexes

Regional security complexes are international subsystems and therefore viewing them as having their own structures and patterns of interaction provides a useful benchmark against which to identify and assess changes in the patterns of regional security.

The structure of a regional security complex, such as the Middle East one includes four key components: first, the boundary of the complex that differentiates it from its neighbors; second, the arrangement of its units (an anarchical security complex requires the existence of two or more states); third, the patterns of enmity and amity among its units; and fourth, the distribution of power among its principal units (Buzan and Wæver 2003, 53). Since security complexes constitute products of an anarchic international system, and they represent durable rather than permanent patterns within such a system, (Buzan, Wæver and de Wilde 1998, 15) the composition and structure of a security complex may change over time if one or more of the four key components change. Hence, major shifts in any of these components would normally require a redefinition of the Middle East security complex.

Four structural options are available for assessing the impact of change on a security complex: maintenance of the status quo, internal transformation, external transformation and overlay (Buzan, Wæver and de Wilde 1998, 18). Maintenance of the status quo means the essential structure of the regional security complex remains fundamentally intact. This does not mean that no change has taken place but rather that the changes that have occurred have tended either to support or not undermine the structure. Internal transformation of a regional security complex occurs when its structure changes as a result of regional political integration, decisive shifts in the distribution of power, or major shifts in the pattern of amity and enmity. External transformation occurs when the structure of a regional security complex is altered by either the expansion or contraction of its existing outer boundary. Minor adjustments to the boundary may not significantly affect the essential structure. The addition or deletion of major states, however, is certain to have a substantial impact on both the distribution of power and the pattern of amity and enmity. Finally, overlay means one or more external powers moves directly into the regional complex with the effect of suppressing the indigenous security dynamic.

Buzan and Wæver (2003, 55) have drawn a distinction between 'standard' and 'centered' regional security complexes. Centered regional security complexes come in three different forms: first, those centered on a superpower (e.g. the US dominates the North and Central America), those centered on a great power (e.g. Russia and the CIS) and those centered on a regional organization that reflects a high degree of regional integration (e.g. the European Union and Europe). A standard regional security complex is composed of two or more states that share a predominantly military and political security agenda. All standard complexes are anarchical in nature. In this sense, the Middle East security complex constitutes a standard security complex.

The Middle East Security Complex

RSCT helps us identify a standard and high-level Middle East security complex which Turkey and Afghanistan help to insulate from the European and South Asia security complexes respectively. Although power relations and patterns of amity and enmity are the main defining factors of the Middle East security complex, cultural, religious and ethnic ties among states also come into play.

Within the Middle East security complex, one can currently identify three sub-complexes.

However, the sub-complexes that are suggested here do not correspond to those identified by Buzan and Wæver. Since the structure of regional security complexes is not permanent and since the patterns of relations among states are dynamic rather than static, it can be argued that the regional relations of the early 2000s (when Buzan and Wæver advanced their argument) have changed. This change has impacted the structure of the Middle East sub-complexes, as well as the Middle East security complex as a whole. Specifically, Buzan and Wæver have correctly suggested that the first and defining core sub-complex in the Middle East is the one centered in the Levant – between Israel and its Arab neighbors – which has given rise to many regional wars. This sub-complex is the result and the reflection of the local struggle between Israel and the Palestinians, which set up and sustained a much wider hostility between Israel, on the one hand, and its immediate neighbors, as well as the wider Arab world, on the other. To a lesser extent, this struggle has been shadowed by a conflict between Israel and the wider Islamic world.

However, a case can be made that the Levant sub-complex also includes the Maghreb states, which Buzan and Wæver have identified as constituting a separate albeit a very weak sub-complex centered on the shifting and uneasy set of relations among Libya, Tunisia, Algeria and Morocco. According to Buzan and Wæver (2003, 193), the main regional security problem in the Maghreb has been the Moroccan annexation of Western Sahara in 1975 – which led to tensions with Libya and Algeria. The argument that the Maghreb countries are currently part of the Levant sub-complex is advanced for two reasons: first, today the Western Sahara issue is not strong enough to provide the basis of a wide Maghreb sub-complex which cannot account for the place of Tunisia; and second, the Maghreb countries together with those of the Levant sub-complex have many things in common. For example, the Maghreb states have had a considerable involvement in the Arab–Israeli conflict, they are members of the Arab League, partners in the European Union's Neighbourhood Policy (ENP), and members of the Euro-Mediterranean Partnership (EMP) and the Union for the Mediterranean (UfM). In other words, the Maghreb sub-complex has experienced internal transformation – while the Levant complex has undergone external transformation by incorporating the Maghreb countries.

As Buzan and Wæver suggest, a strong case can be made that the second sub-complex in the Middle East is the one centered on the triangular rivalry among Iran, Iraq and the Gulf Arab states led by Saudi Arabia. To this core rivalry, one may add the peripheral rivalry between Yemen and Saudi Arabia.

Scholars have suggested (Buzan and Wæver 2003, 155; Clapham 1996, 128; Tibi 1993, 52) that the Horn of Africa sub-complex should be located within the African security complex. However, due to increasing patterns of security interdependence, a strong case can be made that today this sub-complex constitutes a third Middle East sub-complex with Sudan and Somalia as its principals and where Saudi-Arabia, Egypt and the Gulf States have taken a significant interest. Hence the Middle East security complex has undergone external transformation by incorporating the Horn of Africa sub-complex. Since maintenance of the status quo would imply that the essential structure of the Middle East security complex would remain fundamentally intact, we argue that this regional security complex has not been static (since it has undergone both a domestic and external transformation) and therefore its structure has been changed.

Conflict and Diplomacy in the Middle East

The modern Middle East began after the First World War, when the Ottoman Empire was defeated by the British Empire and their allies and partitioned into a number of separate entities, initially under British and French Mandates. The most important regional transformations following the end of the Second World War included the establishment of the state of Israel in 1948, the departure of the colonial powers (Britain and France) from the region by the end of the 1960s, and the rising influence and regional involvement of the US from the 1970s onwards.

During the Cold War, the Middle East was a theater of ideological struggle between the US and the Soviet Union and their respective allies. Among many important areas of contention between the superpowers was their desire to gain strategic advantage in the region and secure access to oil reserves at a time when oil was becoming increasingly vital to the economy of the industrialized countries of the West. Consequently, the US sought to prevent the Arab world from being exposed to Soviet influence.

The collapse of the Soviet Union in the early 1990s had several consequences for the Middle East. First of all, it allowed large numbers of Jewish people to immigrate from Russia and Ukraine to Israel, further strengthening the Jewish state. Second, it cut off the easiest source of credit, armaments, and diplomatic support to the anti-Western Arab regimes, weakening their position. Third, it opened up the prospect of cheap oil from Russia, driving down oil prices and reducing the dependence of the Western world on oil from the Arab states. Fourth, it discredited the model of development through authoritarian state socialism that Egypt (under Nasser), Algeria, Syria, and Iraq had followed since the 1960s – leaving these regimes politically and economically stranded. As a result, regional rulers, such as Iraq's Saddam Hussein increasingly relied on Arab nationalism as a substitute for socialism.

In a bid for regional hegemony, Saddam Hussein invaded Kuwait in 1990. In response, the US formed an international coalition that included Middle East states such as Saudi Arabia, Egypt, and Syria and evicted Iraq from Kuwait. However, the Gulf War later led to a permanent US military presence in the Persian Gulf, particularly in Saudi Arabia (the land where the holy cities of Mecca and Medina are located), which offended many Muslims, and was a reason often cited by Osama bin Laden as justification for the 9/11 attacks.

The change of governance from autocracy to democracy that occurred in many places around the world following the end of the Cold War did not take place in the Middle East. At the same time, in most Middle East countries the growth of market economies was limited by political restrictions, corruption, cronyism, overspending on arms and prestige projects, and over-dependence on oil revenues. The successful economies were those countries that had oil wealth and low populations, such as the Gulf States where the ruling elites allowed some political and social liberalization – but without giving up any of their own power. Lebanon also rebuilt a fairly successful economy after a prolonged civil war in the 1980s. During the 2000s, all these factors intensified conflict in the Middle East, which affected the entire world. The failure of the Clinton Administration to broker a peace deal between Israel and Palestine at the Camp David Summit in 2000 led eventually to the new Intifada that marked the first major outbreak of violence since the 1993 Oslo Peace Accords. At the same time, the failures of most of the Arab regimes and the bankruptcy of secular Arab radicalism led a section of educated Arabs (and other Muslims) to embrace Islamism, promoted (to differing degrees) both by Iran's Shia clerics as well as by Saudi Arabia's powerful Wahhabist movement. Many of the militant Islamists gained their military training while fighting Soviet forces in Afghanistan.

In response to the 9/11 attack, US President George W. Bush decided to invade Afghanistan in 2001 to overthrow the Taliban regime – which had been harboring Bin Laden and al-Qaeda. However, Bush's decision to invade Iraq in 2003 went against the advice of Sunni Middle Eastern states and most notably Saudi Arabia. It led to a prolonged occupation of a Middle Eastern capital by a Western army and marked a turning point in the history of the region. Despite elections held in January 2005, much of Iraq had all but disintegrated due to a post-war insurgency. Many dissatisfied Sunnis who once served in the Iraqi Army under Saddam Hussein were successful in organizing a new organization, namely ISIS. While ISIS has been significantly weakened in the Levant, branches of the organization have spread to other countries outside the Middle East and most notably Africa.

By 2005, the situation between the Israelis and the Palestinians had also deteriorated while in 2006 a new conflict had erupted between Israel and Hezbollah in southern Lebanon – further setting back any prospects for peace in the region. Meanwhile, in 2004, a Shia insurgency had also begun in Yemen. This eventually led to a war, that is still raging at the time of writing, and to the deterioration of Iran–Saudi Arabia relations as both became embroiled in a proxy war in Yemen. Finally, starting in late 2010, the Arab Spring brought major protests, uprisings, and even revolutions to several Middle Eastern countries. This challenged the existing social and political order of the region and eventually led to a prolonged Syrian civil war that has seen the military intervention of Western powers, Russia and many regional states to either support the Syrian opposition groups or the ruling Ba'ath party. All these developments have added to regional complexity, which the contributors to this volume have attempted to unpack.

Book Structure

The volume is divided into 9 chapters. In Chapter 1, Ayşegül Sever examines how the processes of globalization and regionalization condition state attitudes and policies as well as international relations in the Middle East. She argues that given the variety of regionalisms, Middle Eastern regionalism has some commonalities as well as differences compared to similar processes in other regions. She suggests that regionally initiated problem-solving mechanisms have been both weak and dysfunctional in the Middle East mainly as a result of the persistent outside intervention, which, nevertheless, is crucial for the ultimate resolution of critical regional conflicts. Sever points out that the spill over of Middle Eastern problems pose serious global challenges to the extent that what is regional and what is global has become obscure.

In Chapter 2, Onur Erpul investigates whether or not Middle Eastern states are able to obtain a tenable regional order. Approaching the question of regional order from an English School perspective, he explores the conditions that inhibit the moderation of conflict in the region at different levels of analysis. In doing so, he argues that there are numerous, cross-cutting, sources of conflict and disunity in the region including the overbearing presence of extra-regional powers, the lack of a common vision acceptable to all Middle Eastern states, the internal locus of security threats for many states, and the use of non-state violence. He concludes that although there are mitigating circumstances, the Middle East international society is at best in a transitional and conflictive phase.

In Chapter 3, Jonathan Cristol examines key events in US foreign policy in the Middle East after the Cold War including the Persian Gulf War; the Israeli–Palestinian peace process; Osama bin Laden & al-Qaeda; the Arab Spring; the Iranian nuclear program; the Syrian Civil War; and the Gulf Cooperation Council crisis – among others. He argues that although the US did not cause all of the problems currently facing the Middle East, the US has a mixed track record in its response to regional events. He concludes that although President George H.W. Bush's successful use of diplomacy and military power during the 1991 Gulf War presented new and unprecedented opportunities for the region, in the present day the region has fallen into disarray with American leadership more distant than ever.

In Chapter 4, Spyridon N. Litsas scrutinizes Russia's involvement in the Middle East under Putin. He argues that for the first time in Russia's long history Moscow sees the region not as a suitable arena to destabilize Western interests but as a suitable venue to implement its geostrategic plans. He points out that Russia follows a more aggressive and interventionist approach than during the past and yet it maintains the old style of deceit. He concludes that Moscow implements an advanced strategy in the Middle East and whoever is ready to disregard this will be negatively surprised in the years to come.

In Chapter 5, Xi Chen explores the most recent dynamics of China–Middle East relations from an historical context. Chen argues that China has sought to establish and maintain a prominent presence in the region in recent years. However, she maintains Beijing's new grand Arab Policy is yet to come as China's engagement with the region remains primarily driven by its economic interests – while its diplomatic, cultural, and military involvement in the Middle East is still largely symbolic.

In Chapter 6, Stefanie Georgakis Abbott examines the European Union's approach to the Middle East and North Africa (MENA) region by analyzing the institutional framework provided by the Euro-Mediterranean Partnership (EMP) and the Union for the Mediterranean (UfM). In doing so, she points out that the EU seeks to encourage and facilitate political, social, humanitarian, and economic reform in its MENA neighbors; deepen relationships – both bilaterally and regionally – between the EU and its MENA partners as well as between MENA states themselves; and address Israeli–Palestinian relations. She concludes that unlike the EMP, the UfM provides a more pragmatic and inclusive approach to the problems and challenges facing the MENA region.

In Chapter 7, Yannis A. Stivachtis investigates the European Union's approach to the MENA region by focusing on the European Neighborhood Policy (ENP). He argues that despite its rhetoric and revisions, the ENP has failed to produce the expected results mainly because it has discounted the feedback of the MENA countries. Following a 2015 Review, it remains to be seen whether the EU would be open to questions, criticism and suggestions from its MENA partners. It also remains to be seen whether MENA countries would play any role in setting the benchmarks of deep reform, have a say in how relevant EU policies develop, or would be involved in the performance assessment. Stivachtis concludes by noting that a more effective engagement with the MENA region would require the EU to abolish neocolonial attitudes reflecting a 'civilizer–civilizee' relationship and instead be more open to the perceptions and viewpoints of its MENA neighbors – thereby cultivating a relationship of mutual respect and equal partnership with them.

In Chapter 8, Allison Miller investigates the contributions of the United Nations (UN) to Middle East peace and security. She argues that the traditional UN approach to regional security through the use of peacekeeping forces has been recently supplemented by a new approach that emphasizes human security. As a result, the UN has sought to address regional security needs through developmental aid, humanitarian aid, and assistance to vulnerable groups. Miller points out that the Middle East is engulfed in conflict, ranging from civil wars, terrorism, and refugee crises that require and necessitate UN involvement. She concludes that in order to address regional security challenges the UN should continuously work towards building partnerships with leading regional organizations, primarily the Arab League – and that future regional stability depends on the ability of the UN and its partner organizations to protect vulnerable groups and continuously work towards humanitarian and developmental goals.

Finally, in Chapter 9, Ali G. Dizboni and Sofwat Omar investigate Iran's hegemonic aspirations. They argue that a complicated and savage chess game is currently taking place in the Middle East as different countries – including Saudi Arabia, Iran, Turkey, and Israel – are attempting to become the regional hegemon. They suggest that a "Shia Crescent" has been created where Shia forces in Lebanon, Syria, Iraq, and Yemen are supported by the Iranian regime and that with Russian assistance and the removal of international sanctions following the nuclear deal, Iran has positioned itself as the dominant power of the Middle East. They conclude that if the reformist camp is successful, the economy continues to improve, inflation is reduced, and progress continues to be made, then there is a high probability that Iran's aspirations to be a regional hegemon will be successful.

References

Buzan, Barry. 2016. *People, States and Fear: An Agenda for International Security Studies in the Post-Cold War Era.* Reprint. Colchester: ECPR Press.

Buzan, Barry. 1991. *People, States and Fear: An Agenda for International Security Studies in the Post-Cold War Era.* 2nd edition. London: Harvester Wheatscheaf.

Buzan, Barry. 1983. *People, States and Fear: An Agenda for International Security Studies in the Post-Cold War Era.* London: Harvester Wheatscheaf.

Buzan, Barry and Ole Wæver. 2003. *Regions and Powers: The Structure of International Security*. Cambridge: Cambridge University Press.

Buzan, Barry, Wæver, Ole and Jaap de Wilde. 1998. *Security: A New Framework for Analysis*. Boulder, CO: Lynne Rienner.

Clapham, Christopher. 1996. *Africa and the International System*. Cambridge: Cambridge University Press.

Lake David A. and Patrick M. Morgan. 1997. *Regional Orders: Building Security in a New World*. Park, PA: Penn State University Press.

Tibi, Bassim. 1993. *Conflict and War in the Middle East, 1967–1991: Regional Dynamics and the Superpowers*. London: Macmillan.

1

Globalism, Regionalism and the Middle East

AYŞEGÜL SEVER

Regionalism and globalism are two of the leading phenomena in world politics. In the age of globalism, regionalism can be treated as a complementary and interacting phenomenon – or as a competing and conflicting one. Globalization creates powerful demands for regionalism that are not particular to one specific region, but to all regions. Considering the global-regional nexus as an unavoidably synchronized and complimentary set of processes concerning the Middle East, the chapter primarily draws attention to the state of regionalism in the Arab Middle East and its spillovers. With nationalist and protectionist trends on the rise with the election of Donald Trump in the US and the UK's Brexit decision, it is perhaps not a popular time for commenting on the state of regionalism in the Middle East. A scarcity of regional cooperation in the area has also led interested commentators and scholars to label the Middle East as "the region without regionalism" (Aarts 1999, 91) or a space of weak regionalism.

The Middle East is often viewed as exceptional, resisting global trends of economic and political liberalism as well as regionalism in the age of globalization (Hazbun 2012, 207–208). Having said that, regionalism in the Middle East continues to be a part of wider scholarly debate on regionalism with different perspectives and approaches. When treating regionalism as a positive phenomenon – leading to economic, political and security cooperation in a geographically defined area – it is expected to conform to the needs of global governance. How much this could be the case for the Middle East in the current stage of regionalism in the area will be one of the major themes explored in this chapter. In the presence of various regionalisms, Middle East regionalism has some commonalities and differences compared to Asia, Africa or Latin America. As with other regions, the Middle East is a constructed region whose boundaries and the level of its *region-ness* are open to discussion, especially in the absence of significant degrees of institutionalization or a definition of common norms and identities. In this chapter, the most common form of geographical definition of the Middle East which is bounded with all the Arab states and three non-Arab states – namely, Israel, Iran and Turkey – is accepted, but the Arab Middle East will be the center of attention.

There are a large number of studies indicating how weak regionalism has always been in the Middle East due to issues such as a lack of democracy, the absence of regional hegemony, and the non-existence of economic interdependence. A general consensus prevails that the Middle East has not been a successful example of regional cooperation or regional integration over the years. Almost all forms of regional initiatives aiming at conflict resolution, democracy promotion or creating a common market have mainly failed. Recent Middle Eastern problems are posing more global challenges than perhaps the sum of other regional challenges – demonstrating the centrality of the region to the wider world. In other words, what is regional and what is global have become obscure given that the Syrian civil war, in particular, opened Pandora's box with the worldwide challenges of transborder armed groups, migration, human rights abuses, and failed states.

In the early days of the Arab Spring post-2010, the diffusion effects of what happened, in Tunisia particularly, raised some expectations about whether the Middle East would see the beginning of a new era of regional cooperation. Instead, it seems that the further weakening of the Arab state system has given rise to new transnational identities such as tribalism, sectarianism and ethnicism – rather than regional unity. Instead of seeing the growing interconnectedness as a result of flows of capital, labor, and common democratic values, there have been challenging spillovers of conflicts and civil wars. Having said that, despite these established pessimistic views, in recent years some studies have begun to address Middle East regionalism rather differently by focusing on non-state actors and emphasizing the significance of ongoing networks and interactions in assessing the new possibilities of bottom-up regionalization. In other words, assessing Middle East regionalism on its own terms rather than comparing it with other regionalisms. After outlining the conceptual framework that will be applied to regionalism in the Arab Middle East, the chapter briefly revisits the most common arguments about what went wrong with Middle East regionalism. It then looks at regionalism in the Arab Middle East in the light of existing institutional forms of regionalism – while taking new multidimensional perspectives of regionalism into account.

Framing Regionalism in the Middle East

The definition of "region" is essential for any regional analysis including that of the Middle East. There has been a tendency to deemphasize the geographic elements of regions while focusing on political and ideational characters. Thus, according to Katzenstein, regions are "socially constructed and politically contested" (1997, 7). In defining regions, scholars underscore various characteristics for being or becoming a region. For instance, Russett emphasized factors such as geographical proximity, social and cultural homogeneity, political institutions, and economic interdependence (1967, 11). On the other hand, Cantori and Spiegel (1970, 6–7) regard geographical contiguity, common historical, cultural, and linguistic bonds as well as international interactions as a necessity for the definition of a region. Based on these definitions, where the Middle East stands is not clear.

Considering cultural and religious commonalities, the Middle East has the potential for being regarded as a region. For example, in the Arab Human Development Report 2002, it is suggested that "perhaps no other group of states in the world has been endorsed with the same potential for cooperation, even integration, as have the Arab countries" (UNDP 2002, 121) given that the area has a common historical experience and Arab-Muslim identity represents a relatively high degree of cultural, religious, and linguistic homogeneity. The region has also been identified by a significant degree of interaction witnessed in extensive family ties across borders, and the presence of transnational actors including Islamists, migrants, and business communities (Legrenzi and Harders 2008, 2). Moreover, the emergence of a well-integrated Arab media market has also created an Arab public space. On the other hand, when examining economic interdependence or creating common norm and values, it is hard to resolve the capacity of the Middle East for region-ness. As in most regions of the world, the Middle East was first framed by strategic considerations and military concerns. The Middle East also had its roots in "the security conceptions and practices which were imposed or invented by Western powers" (Bilgin 2004, 26). Considering Europe's colonial and imperial past, the imposition of the Cold War and the War on Terror, it is hard to separate the idea of the Middle East "from the power and the knowledge created and imposed by the West on the rest of the world" (Gasper 2012, 240). Given this, Gasper argues that the Middle East exists "because the West has possessed sufficient power to give the idea substance" (2012, 240).

The Middle East is, then, an externally invented region. It was first mentioned in name in an article entitled "The Persian Gulf and International Relations," by American naval strategist Alfred Thayer Mahan in 1902 who signified the strategic value of the region for British imperial needs (Adelson 2012, 37). The term Middle East was used in the Second World War by the British, for the first time, when they called their contingent in Egypt the Middle East Command. At the time, Britain had troops as far as China and also as close as Western Europe. In view of this, British forces in Egypt remained somewhere in the middle in terms of closeness to Britain. So, the term Middle East was a descriptive one for the British and eventually became ubiquitous. Since then, the response to how the region has been constructed in the interplay between various types of state, market and civil society actors remains ambiguous. Reconstructing or deconstructing of the Middle East remains an open question. External initiatives such as the Euro-Mediterranean Partnership or the Greater Middle East have taken their turn, but with no success. On the other hand, the uprisings of the Arab Spring signaled that possible regionalized interactions through networking or other means call for new interpretations of regionalism in the Middle East.

In view of the above, looking at the state of regionalism in the Middle East from the New Regionalism Approach (NRA) perspective could be more promising to comprehend current and future forms of regionalism – or at least to review some of the common pessimistic accounts. The new regionalism approach is generally defined as a comprehensive, multidimensional, and political phenomenon – including all different varieties of issues including economy, security, culture, and environment (Hettne 1999, 19). The NRA's definition of the region as a space open to reconstruction and its acceptance of multiplicity of the actors and different forms of regionalism give a better perspective to look at the Arab Middle East. Consequently, looking at various forms of regionalism in addition to state-led regionalism could be better matched to inquiry about regionalism in the Middle East. Even though there are ample works examining the problems of top-down weak regionalism in the Middle East, there are also recent studies emphasizing the significance of networks, interactions and transnational movements in assessing regionalism, and new possibilities of regionalization in the area (Ferabolli 2015; Valbjorn 2016). Some of these movements are led by classical interstate organizations such as the Arab League, while others are more ad hoc transregional processes. Concurrently, some distinctions made in the literature about regional cooperation – such as regionalism and regionalization – could be of use in the context of the Arab Middle East.

There is a broad consensus in the literature that regionalism in the Middle East in the meaning of social, political cohesiveness or economic interdependence – or the existence of region-wide institutions – is not a strong phenomenon. The absence of viable states, the authoritarian nature of Arab states, ongoing issues like the Arab–Israeli conflict, and external intervention are generally accepted as the causes which make the process of region building in the Middle East difficult to achieve. Taking all these into account, regionalism in the area would be better treated very widely since it may incorporate regional groups and networks as well as interstate arrangements and organizations. A regionalism/regionalization division could be beneficial to better comprehend the Middle East in regionalism studies. In discussing the multifaceted experience of regionalism in various regions, regionalism and regionalization are the two concepts which are often used to signify different forms and stages of regional cooperation and interactions. These two concepts are interwoven and hard to differentiate, but regionalization and regionalism are perceived differently in terms of involving actors, their occurrence with top-down or bottom-up initiatives, and their attention to the outcome or procedure. Regionalism is generally understood as a state-led or states-led project designed to reorganize particular regional space along defined economic, institutional, and political lines. Regionalization, on the other hand, defines more spontaneous and endogenous processes which involve "undirected economic and social interactions between non-state actors whether individuals, firms, companies, NGOs, etc." (Legrenzi 2013, 1). Having said that, there is no such a thing as state led regionalism versus non-state led regionalism.

The distinctive aspect of the NRA is its effort to bring non-state actors and informal processes into the purview of regionalism studies. Some define regionalization as a looser form of regionalism or soft regionalism (Behr and Jokela 2011, 5). All these indicate that regionalism is an increasingly complex and diverse phenomenon that is used to describe various levels of interaction among a broad set of regional actors. Regional orders encompass both regionalization and regional institution building. The question is therefore not so much whether regionalism will endure, but what kind of shape it will take in the emerging global order. Many regional groupings consciously started avoiding the institutional and bureaucratic structure of traditional organizations, but old forms of regionalism such as interstate organization did not disappear either. New functions and roles were incorporated into their former standing and status (Hettne and Söderbaum 2008, 66). Moreover, civil society and state apparatus need to come together in a variety of networks and regional schemes and they also do this to some extent in the context of the Arab Middle East. Any well functioning regionalist project needs to have a linkage between state and non-state actors (Fawcett 2004, 433). As a result, the NRA takes into account both state and non-state actors with a focus on both formal and informal processes of regionalization.

Varying Forms of Regionalism in the Arab Middle East

Formal institutional forms of regionalism in the Arab Middle East are embodied in several organizations among which the Arab League and the Gulf Cooperation Council (GCC) will be taken into account. Both are forms of state-driven regional cooperation, but do not represent a profound kind of economic and political integration. Other than their rare contribution to regional cooperation, these organizations generally remain incompetent in resolving regional crises or enabling reliable regional cooperation. Regional organizations are supposed to contribute to conflict resolution, the formation of a common market, and the consolidation of democracy and human rights. But, these have hardly been achieved in the Middle East. However, it would be too far reaching to exclude them altogether as players of regionalism in the Arab Middle East. Ferabolli suggests that they still at least could provide relevant platforms for the growing exchanges in Arab society and therefore also indirectly contribute to the regionalization of the Arab Middle East (Ferrabolli 2016, 189). As regards security and conflict-resolution, there are some cases where the Arab League has played a role, but no final solution has been accomplished. The League, for instance, played a mediating role in the Kuwait–Iraq crisis in 1961, Algeria's invasion of Morocco in 1963, and provided regional support to the intervention in Libya during the Arab Spring. Nonetheless, instead of providing a regional solution, the Arab League has often remained ineffective due to internal rivalries during regional crises such as the 1990–1991 Gulf crisis, the 2003 Iraq War and the 2009 Gaza conflict (Valbjorn 2016). Other than the Israel issue, the League members are rarely united on critical issues. The Arab Middle East is therefore widely accepted as one of the least regionally integrated or institutionalized areas of the world.

The first formal regional organization in the Middle East – the Arab League – came into being in 1945 and became the first regional organization in the Third World. The Arab League was initially founded by Egypt, Iraq, Jordan, Lebanon, Saudi Arabia, Syria, and Yemen. It currently has 22 member states and is based on a shared culture and language with the aim to serve the common good of all Arab countries. However, as Barnett points out, shared identities do not necessarily promote regional cooperation as long as inward-looking state survival takes priority (Barnett and Solingen 2007, 213). For example, having the feeling of *Arabness* did not lead to a common understanding about common norms that each Arab state should adopt. Even a strong appeal of Arab nationalism (Pan-Arabism) during Nasser's reign did not bring about cross national unity since the state-centered approach in the Arab world remained persistent. Most of the regional organizations, including the Arab League, were awarded with only limited autonomy by the member states who preferred to retain power at the nation-state level. Consequently, the existing cooperation among the authoritarian states of the Arab League is defined as "regime boosting regionalism" where the status, the legitimacy, and the general interests of authoritarian regimes are strengthened through the League at the expense of genuine regional cooperation (Börzel and Risse

2016). Between 1945 and 1970 Pan-Arabism became the basis for regional organizations and cooperative projects in the region. However, this Arab discourse was not transformed into practical outcomes (Schulz and Schulz 2005, 191). Rather than progress along the lines of Pan-Arabism, nationalism and the promotion of state interests gained the upper hand over regionalism based on common culture.

The Arab League has traditionally been a club of authoritarian Arab states (Valbjorn 2016). This situation is evident in the Freedom House reports which consistently rate the Middle East as the most authoritarian in the world (Brynen and Moore 2013, 4). With regard to this situation, Tripp states that leaders who are unwilling to make compromises with domestic constituencies appear similarly unwilling to make compromises with neighboring states (Tripp 1981, 302). In the context of Arab unity, the Arab world therefore aimed at creating an organization that would preserve state sovereignty. Therefore, the prominence of the principle of non-interference and unanimity in the charter of the Arab League is not a coincidence (Beck 2015, 195–96). These principles prevented the organization from taking an effective action in the case of major regional conflicts. How reversible these principles have become came under scrutiny when the unanimity and interference principles were overlooked by Saudi Arabia during its intervention in Yemen since 2015. Despite its serious weaknesses in capacity and fulfillment, the League occasionally took significant steps in some issues such as promotion of education. Other steps such as the establishment of a Human Rights Committee were also taken following the Arab Charter on Human Rights in 2008. However, such efforts remained superficial and the League did not sincerely engage in a debate about political liberalization and democratization even after the Arab Spring (Valbjorn 2016). Thus, the Charter on Human Rights was generally regarded as a tentative move to preclude outside intervention in domestic and regional affairs.

During some critical periods, regional and global developments required some changes and adjustments for the state of regionalism in the Middle East. The period following the 1967 war or the period after the Arab Spring are examples of this. The 1967 Arab–Israeli war ended the revolutionary state-led Pan-Arabism under Nasser but also marked the beginning of a new kind of Arab regionalism. The oil boom in the early 1970s brought about new forms of social and economic interconnectedness in the Arab world with flows of workers from poorer Arab countries into the oil-rich ones (Legrenzi and Herders 2013, 2). On the other hand, capital via remittances, investments, and aid started to go in the opposite direction. This circulation resulted in new economic exchanges as well as the share of ideas and values, which created a new sense of belonging in a larger Arab community. By the end of the 1970s, millions of Arab migrants moved to the current Gulf Cooperation

Council (GCC) countries (Ferabolli 2016, 41). This was not a sign of growing regional economic integration as economic relations generally remained in the form of labor movement and remittances at the sub-regional or bilateral level.

As has been the case with political issues, regional leaders have been often hesitant to surrender power to a regional economic community. The Arab Middle East is, therefore, still generally regarded one of the least economically integrated regions in the world. Low integration with the global economy and the domination of state entrepreneurship have hindered the rise of a private entrepreneurial class across the region (Barnett and Solingen 2007, 184). Intraregional trade in the Arab Middle East is also low and the region's global share of non-oil exports is marginal (Schulz and Schulz 2005, 189). The trade pattern largely consists of agriculture and raw materials, displaying a lack of complementarity. The large differences in GDP per capita among the Gulf states and the rest of the Arab countries is also regarded as one of the reasons for failing economic unity (Seeberg 2016). Attempts to institutionalize regional trade and economic relationships with the initiatives such as the Agadir Agreement, the GCC Customs Union, the North African Union, and the Arab Maghreb Union (AMU) have all failed to create an integrated regional economy. The Arab League's foremost project, the Greater Arab Free Trade Area (GAFTA), launched in 1997 also fell short of providing integrated trade relations in the region (Vignal 2017).

The rise of sub-regionalisms in the Gulf or North Africa in the 1980s also brought about a new dimension to reassess state-led regionalism at a different level in the Middle East. The most famous example of sub-regionalism in the region is the GCC which includes Saudi Arabia, Kuwait, Bahrain, Qatar, the UAE, and Oman and was established in 1981 in the wake of the Iranian revolution of 1979. Despite all its shortcomings, the GCC is regarded as the most successful example of regionalism in the Middle East especially in the context of other examples of sub-regionalism in the region. Compared to the other sub-regionalisms, the GCC is moving towards the consolidation of a common market and a monetary union. The Arab Maghreb Union (AMU) was also set up in 1989 with the involvement of Algeria, Libya, Mauritania, Morocco, and Tunisia to provide economic and social progress with the free circulation of goods and people in North Africa. Among other sub-regionalist projects, the AMU emerged as a response to the growing integration in Europe by aiming at creating a customs union along the same lines as the European Community. However, it was destined to fail in view of consistent political quarrels among member states and the members giving priority to their bilateral relations with the European Union over intra-AMU economic integration.

Other than the abovementioned organizational regionalisms, the presence of civil society and growing transnational exchanges in the region leads many to consider the extent of regionalism in the Arab Middle East in the context of regionalization. In the 1980s and 1990s, civil society and networks of civil society activism in the Middle East came to the forefront. The liberal waves of the 1990s – the globalization of the ideas of human rights, political participation, and market economy – opened up new spaces for social mobilization in the Middle East. All sorts of NGOs mushroomed in the region. They became critically important in expressing the common people's needs and also formed "the social safety net that every country requires" (Gubser 2002, 140). UNDP Arab Human Development Reports consider the emergence of civil society as a significant factor of human development progress (Isfahani 2010). The regional conjecture also affected the rise of some other important issues. For example, in the 1990s when the signing of the Oslo Accords between the Israeli and Palestinian leadership created an atmosphere of hope, a civil society initiative – the Alliance for Middle East Peace (ALLMEP) – assembled 44 NGOs promoting coexistence between Arabs and Jews in the Middle East (Krokowska 2010, 41). Another large gathering also took place in Cairo in 1997 when 700 NGO representatives from all parts of the Arab world came together to exchange their views and projects on population and development (Bayat 2002, 15). Over a range of transnational and global issues, Arab networks are working together. For example, there are numerous Arab Networks for environment, human rights, and development issues that share knowledge, expertise, and projected solutions.

Civil society activism has been comparatively stronger in some Arab countries – such as Egypt, Jordan, and Palestine – than in others. The donors of NGOs in these countries have generally been rich Arab countries (Gubser 2002, 146). They also receive financial and technical assistance from international NGOs (INGOs). The emergence of a dynamic civil society in the Middle East was initially, especially in the early 1990s, regarded as a good sign of democratization – especially when the transition to democracy was taking place in various parts of the world after the collapse of the Soviet Union in 1991. It was expected that an 'awakening of civil society' would lead the Arab world to democratization as it had done so for Eastern Europe (Kubba 2000, 84–90). Therefore, civil society assistance "has constituted the linchpin of international MENA democracy promotion efforts" in the 1990s (Yom 2005, 17). Even though the confluence of domestic and global trends brought about significant civil society activism, all were ineffective challenges to state authoritarianism. As a result, state intervention and manipulation of civil society continue to be a serious problem across the Middle East. Arab civil society may be stronger compared to earlier periods, but "the state remains far more powerful" in most cases (Carapico 2000, 14). As national civil society organizations, transnational forums have also remained either under the direct control of "respective governments as government organized NGOs or operate within tight governmental supervision" (Pinfari 2014, 166). Consequently, regional civil society actors still seem to play a regional role to the extent that state-based regionalism allows them to. Therefore, in the Arab Middle East, the top down and bottom up regional discursive practices are intertwined.

Despite all the problems and complexities involved, bottom-up regionalization is very much at work. "Open and horizontal" features of social media also provide previously marginalized groups such as youth, women and ethnic minorities in the MENA region with a new "Arab public sphere" (Gheytanchi and Moghadam 2014, 6). All sorts of people and social actors are on the move in the region – on a voluntary basis as well as due to necessity. There is a growing interaction among Arab societies on voluntary basis to work, travel, and get better education or health services. For example, labor mobility within the Arab world is still one of the significant drivers of regional economic and social integration. For example, the presence of Palestinians in the Gulf helped the "transmission of ideas and building of activist organizations" (Ferabolli 2016, 136).

Turning to tourism, the role of the Arab Tourist Organization, an NGO in Saudi Arabia, has been pivotal in the rise of intra-Arab tourism (Ferabolli 2016, 145–46). Intra-regional student mobility is also growing because of equal enrolment policies for every Arab student as well as a common language of instruction (Ferabolli 2016, 148). At this juncture, one could mention some NGO networks such as the Association of Arab Universities as a relevant contributor to regional cooperation in education. The diffusion of ideas and culture through satellite and Pan-Arab broadcasting has also been crucial in the region (Vignal 2017). While considering the importance of Arab media in the creation of regional belonging, it is hard to distinguish the roles of formal and informal forms of regionalism. It is almost impossible to talk about the new media in the Arab world without reference to the role of the Arab League in the formation of Arabsat and the role of the GCC states in financing it (Ferabolli 2016, 156). Another example is seen in the Arab film industry. To get funding for a film to partake in Arab film festivals requires being a citizen of an Arab League member state (Ferabolli 2016, 173). The regionalization of the cultural productions in the Arab world such as Arab literature and cinema are continuing to make Arab peoples more and more aware of the Arab regional space. Arab states, institutions, and citizens are intersecting in the making of Arab regional politics.

Conflict has also become an important cause of increasing mobility of people from all social classes and professions. For example, a series of regional crises have enforced a new form of regionalization via growing number of refugees. In times of necessity, Iraqis, Syrians and Palestinians flee to the borders of their Arab neighbors which incites the dynamics of regional belonging. The neighboring countries of the conflict regions in the Middle East face large numbers of forced migrants. Moreover, regionalization in the form of expanding cross border radicalization is on the rise. Both cooperative and conflictive regional dynamics are simultaneously in play. Regionalization driven by civil wars, refugees, and transnational identities based on sectarianism poses a novel set of regionalism debates as to the Middle East – with global consequences.

In recent times, the Arab Spring led to a revisiting of all forms of regionalism in the area. Looking at how unexpectedly the people took to the streets during the Arab Spring protests in one country after another, the picture initially displayed hope about the future of Middle East regionalism. The region-wide protests, the searching for democracy and a better life against repression resulted in synchronized protest in quite a number of Arab states. The street protests displayed how regionalization of the Arab Middle East is on the rise when unprecedented region-wide protests with the involvement of various transnational networks and region-wide interactions appear. The uprisings did not cause a transformation to democracy or regional solidarity for the overall change of the status quo. Instead, the authoritarian state mechanism survived and even worsened in some cases. On the other hand, the unprecedented feeling of togetherness among the masses gave hope about the possibility of forming a basis of a long-term cooperation with the participation of multiple actors through interaction. Traditional, long standing, civil society groups were not as active as expected in anti-regime demonstrations during the Arab Spring. Other than the classical organized form of civil society such as NGOs, new forms of civil society activism were observed with the new name 'activated citizenship' throughout the protests (Cavatorta 2012, 78). It became evident that there were numerous modes of engagement ranging from blog writing, artistic expression or mass participation to non-political events (Cavatorta 2012, 81). The Arab world never seemed more unified than during the protests of the Arab Spring with the wave of transnational diffusion in the Arab world.

Following the Arab uprisings in March 2011, the Arab League and the GCC have also reassessed their standings and tried to improve their image – or adjusted themselves to the changing political dynamics of the region. Some even argue that the Arab uprisings triggered a revitalization of regional organizations, particularly the Arab League and the GCC (Beck 2015, 190). Firstly, Libya's League membership, and then Syria's, were suspended. With Libya's suspension, the League took a radical decision to get involved in the internal affairs of a member state by taking the matter to the UN Security

Council. This resulted in UN Resolutions 1970 and 1973 which authorized intervention against the Qaddafi regime through military means. Despite this unusual over-involvement, the League was gradually sidelined by superior US and European involvements including massive NATO bombardment of Libya. In the case of Syria, the Arab league was again quite active with the decision to suspend Syrian membership after Assad's policy towards Syrian civilians and also dispatched joint observer missions with the UN in 2012 and 2013 (Mohamedou 2016, 1225). While it did fall short in forwarding an Arab solution to either the Syrian or ISIS crises, the security concerns of Arab states seemed to be taking a new turn. Consequently, the Arab League announced the creation of a joint military force comprising some 40,000 troops in 2015 (Mohamedou 2016, 1229). In the meantime, the GCC launched campaigns such as an intervention in Bahrain showcasing hard means of security rather than societal instruments of security.

These examples show that conventional nation-state centered understandings of politics in the Middle East fail to capture the realities on the ground. In reality, political and military developments in almost all critical regional issues are heavily influenced by the acts of several non-state actors including Hamas, Hezbollah, ISIS, Jabhat Fatah al-Sham, PKK and PYD. The proliferation of non-state actors, transnational armed groups, the rise of multilayered tribal, and sectarian identity beyond the state request new forms of organizations and cooperation for democracy, development, and security in the region.

Conclusion

While the Middle East might not be a region without regionalism, it seems that any expectations that high levels of regionalization would translate into an advanced regionalism have not been matched by the realities on the ground, yet. In many cases, regionalism in the Arab Middle East remains closely tied to the intensification of insecurity or the consolidation of authoritarian regimes rather than to a cooperation for prosperity, conflict resolution, or democracy. Meanwhile, the Arab League and the GCC frequently underperform and often remain ineffectual. The Middle East is therefore still not a region easily associated with cooperation or integration and is undoubtedly one of the most volatile zones in the world, dominated by crises, conflicts, and wars. Having said that, the potential for cooperation and integration should not be overlooked, and the low level of regionalism should not be taken as a static phenomenon – especially since the protests of the Arab Spring suggested otherwise with the display of unprecedented degrees of regionalization. For the foreseeable future, multifaceted novel forms of regionalism seem to make their appearance with multilayered levels of regional cooperation, transnational diffusion or unwanted forms of regionalization in the region. Considering all the uncertainties and challenges ahead for the region, we would do well to revisit Fawcett's reminder that "there is no ideal region, nor any single agenda to which all regions aspire. Regions, like states, are of varying compositions, capabilities and aspirations" (2004, 434).

References

Aarts, Paul. 1999. "The Middle East: A Region without Regionalism or the End of Exceptionalism?" *Third World Quarterly,* 20, no.5 (October): 911–925.

Adelson, Roger. 2012. "British and US Use and Misuse of the Term Middle East." In *Is There a Middle East: The Evolution of a Geopolitical Concept*, edited by Bonine, Michael E. and others, 36–56. Stanford: Stanford University Press.

Barnett, Michael and Etel Solingen. 2007. "Designed to Fail or Failure to Design? The Origins and Legacy of the Arab League." In *Crafting Cooperation: Regional International Institutions in Comparative Perspective*, edited by Amitav Acharya and Alistair Iain Johnston, 180–221. Cambridge: Cambridge University Press.

Bayat, Asef. 2002. "Activism and Social Development in the Middle East." *International Journal of Middle East Studies*, 34, no. 1 (February): 1–28.

Beck, Martin. 2015. "The End of Regional Middle Eastern Exceptionalism? The Arab League and the Gulf Cooperation Council after the Arab Uprisings," *Democracy and Security,* 11, no. 2 (June): 190–207.

Behr, Timo and Juha Jokela. 2011. "Regionalism and Global Governance: The Emerging Agenda." *Notre Europe Study*, 85 Research 5. http://www.institutdelors.eu/media/regionalism_globalgovernance_t.behr-j.jokela_ne_july2011_01.pdf?pdf=ok.

Bilgin, Pınar. 2004. "Whose 'Middle East'? Geopolitical Inventions and Practices of Security," International Relations 18, no. 1 (March): 25–41.

Börzel, Tanja A. and Thomas Risse. 2016. "Three Cheers for Comparative Regionalism." In *The Oxford Handbook of Comparative Regionalism*, edited by Tanja A. Börzel and Thomas Risse.
Oxford: Oxford University Press.

Brynen, Rex and Pete W. Moore. 2013. "New Horizons in Arab Politics." In *Beyond the Arab Spring: Authoritarianism and Democratization in the Arab World*. New York: Lynne Rienner.

Cantouri, Louis J. and Steven L. Spiegel. 1970. *The International Politics of Regions: A Comparative Approach*. New York: Englewood Cliffs.

Carapico, Sheila. 2000. "NGOs, INGOs, GO-NGOS and Do-NGOs: Making sense of Non-governmental Organizations," *Middle East Report*, 1, no. 1 (September): http://scholarship.richmond.edu/cgi/viewcontent.cgi?article=1001&context=polisci-faculty-publications

Cavatorta, Francesco. 2012. "Arab Spring: The Awakening of Civil Society. A General Overview," *IEMedObs Dossier*: 78, http://www.iemed.org/observatori-en/arees-danalisi/arxius-adjunts/anuari/med.2012/Cavatorta_en.pdf.

Fawcett, Louise. 2004. "Exploring Regional Domains: A Comparative History of Regionalism," *International Affairs*, 80, no. 3 (May): 429–446.

Ferabolli, Silvia. 2015. *Arab Regionalism: A Post-Structural Perspective*. New York: Routledge.

Gasper, Michael Ezekiel. 2012. "Conclusion: There is a Middle East, edited by Bonine, Michael E. and others," In *Is There a Middle East: The Evolution of a Geopolitical Concept*, 231–243. Stanford: Stanford University Press.

Gheytanchi, Elham and Valentine N. Moghadam. 2014. "Women, Social Protests, and the New Media Activism in the Middle East and North Africa," *International Review of Modern Sociology*, 40, no.1 (Spring): 1–26.

Gubser, Peter. 2002. "The Impact of NGOs on State and Non-state Relations in the Middle East," *Middle East Policy*, 9, no. 1 (March): 139–148.

Hazbun, Waleed. 2012. "The Middle East through the Lens of Critical Geopolitics: Globalization, Terrorism and the Iraq War." In *Is there a Middle East: The Evolution of a Geopolitical Concept*, edited by Michael E. Bonine and others, 207–230. Stanford: Stanford University Press.

Hettne, Björn. 1999. "The New Regionalism: A Prologue." In *Globalism and the New Regionalism*, edited by Björn Hettne and others, xv-xxxi. (New York: Macmillan Press, 1999), 19.

Hettne, Björn and Frederick Söderbaum. 2008. "The Future of Regionalism: old divides, new frontiers." In *Regionalization and Global Governance: The Taming of Globalization?*, edited by Andrew F. Cooper and Others, 61–80. Abingdon: Routledge.

Katzenstein, J. Peter. 1997. "Introduction: Asian Regionalism in Comparative Perspective." In *Network Power: Japan and Asia*, edited by J. Peter Katzenstein and Takashi Shiraishi, 1–47. Ithaca N.Y: Cornell University Press.

Kubba, Laith. 2000. "The Awakening of Civil Society," *Journal of Democracy*, 11, no. 3 (July): 84–90.

Krokowska, Katarzyna. 2010. *Cooperation Among Adversaries: Regionalism in the Middle East*, MA Thesis.

Legrenzi, Matteo and Cilja Harders. 2008. "Introduction" In *Beyond Regionalism? Regional Cooperation, Regionalism and Regionalization in the Middle East*, edited by Matteo Legrenzi and Cilja Harders, 1–13. Abingdon: Ashgate.

Legrenzi, Matteo. 2013. "Regionalism and Regionalization in the Middle East: Options and Challenges", IPI Paper (March): 1–12. https://www.ipinst.org/wp-content/uploads/publications/ipi_e_pub_regionalism_me.pdf.

Mohamedou, Muhammed Mahmoud Ould. 2016. "Arab Agency and the UN Project: The League of Arab States between Universality and Regionalism." *Third World Quarterly*, 37, no. 7 (April): 1219–1233.

Pinfari, Marco. 2014. "Transnational Civil Society and Regionalism in the Arab World: More of the Same?" In *Civil Society and World Regions*, edited by Lorenzo Fioramont and others, 161–177. Maryland: Lexington.

Russett, Bruce M. 1970. *International Regions and International Systems*. Chicago: Rand-McNally.

Salehi-Isfahani, Djavad. 2010. Human Development Research Paper 26, https://core.ac.uk/download/pdf/6280411.pdf.

Schulz, Helena and Michael Schulz. 2005. "The Middle East: Regional Instability and Fragmentation." In *Global Politics of Regionalism, Theory and Practice*, edited by Björn Hettne, 187–202. London: Pluto Press.

Seeberg, Peter. 2016. "Analysing Security Subcomplexes in a Changing Middle East-the Role of Non-Arab State Actors and Non-State Actors," *Palgrave Communications*, 2, art. no. 16087.

Tripp, Charles. 1981. "Regional Organizations in the Arab Middle East." In *Regionalism in World Politics*. Oxford: Oxford University Press.

Valbjorn, Morten. 2016. "North Africa and the Middle East." In *The Oxford Handbook of Comparative Regionalism*, edited by Tanja A. Börzel and Thomas Risse. Oxford: Oxford University Press.

Vignal, Leila. 2017. "Transforming Geographies of the Middle East in Times of Globalisation and Uprisings." In *The Transnational Middle East: People, Places, Borders*. New York: Routledge.

UN Human Development Report (UNDP). 2002. http://hdr.undp.org/sites/default/files/reports/263/hdr_2002_en_complete.pdf.

Yom, Sean L. 2005. "Civil Society and Democratization in the Arab World." *Meria Journal*, 9, no. 4 (December): 14–33.

2

The Challenges to Middle Eastern International Society: A Study in Disorder

ONUR ERPUL

When assessing the development of regional peace and cooperation, few areas are as challenging and ambivalent as the Middle East. Europe, the birth place of the modern global international society, enjoys a stable peace. Latin America is characterized by a "long peace;" and most of Africa has witnessed very little interstate war (Bull and Watson 1985; Herbst 2000; Centeno 2002). In this respect, the Middle East is somewhat of an outlier in contemporary international relations as a region marred by both frequent interstate and intrastate conflicts. Although international societies do not abolish wars per se, they do help to tame interstate conflict. This anomalous situation calls into question whether the Middle East comprises an international society. The formal inquiry is thus: to what extent does this society limit the use of force, facilitate conflict resolution, and, most importantly, provide a semblance of order?

According to one of the most authoritative studies of the Middle East from the perspective of international society and order, the Middle East features sufficiently distinct qualities to qualify as a regional society of states with its own unique sub-regional order (Buzan and González-Pelaèz, 2009). However, it remains an unstable space in which the possibility of war has not been eliminated. Moreover, the Middle East has experienced significant political upheaval since the publication of this volume, including the Arab Spring, intensification of Sunni–Shia conflict, the rise of the so-called Islamic State (hereafter ISIS, also known as Daesh and ISIL), fragmentation of important states such as Iraq and Syria, and the growth and diversification of the illicit economic activities in the region. The purpose of this chapter is therefore to examine, update, and in some cases, reinforce existing English school insights on the Middle East by way of examining the relative absence of peace – and even "productive" war (Tilly 1992). On this point, this chapter argues that Middle Eastern international society, to the extent that it can say it preserves a stable order, is relatively weak due primarily to the interference of extra-regional great powers, the absence of a unifying vision of regional order among its diverse members, the institutional fragility of Middle Eastern states, and the prominence of violent illicit non-state actors, all of which provide means and incentives for states to pursue their narrow self-interests without sufficient regard for the broader interests of all regional states. In other words, despite overwhelming historical, civilizational, and even political affinities among Middle Eastern states, the region is characterized today by a relatively underdeveloped international society that is matched by the dysfunction of its interstate system. The chapter's main contention is that Middle Eastern states have failed to define a *raison de système* due in part to the elusiveness of relevant intrastate commonalities.

After introducing the idea of "order" as a theoretical referent to frame Middle Eastern regional politics, the chapter will explore the problems of extra-regional interference in the region's affairs, the cross-cutting conflict between Sunni and Shia states and their numerous proxies, and the persistent problem of state weakness, all of which have served to exacerbate problems such as transnational terrorism, proxy wars, illicit industries, and ethnic as well as sectarian conflict.

Regional Orders and the English School

Before delving into the matter of order in the Middle East, some conceptual clarifications are needed. By order, the present analysis refers to a stable pattern of relations among states in an international society that preserves the common interests of its constituent members despite the deleterious effects of international anarchy (Bull 1977, 1–3). There are different interpretations in the IR lexicon as to how states can achieve their primary objectives under such structural conditions. The English school, which serves as the analytical referent in this chapter, offers a via media between realist and liberal approaches by underscoring states' interests, or *raison d'état*, by manifesting as a commonly-held vision of regional order, which, by virtue of being upheld, can sustain the interests of all its constituent members. This concern for the functioning of international society as a way of serving one's own interests is known as raison de système (Watson 1990, 104–105).

Within the English school, institutions are considered as the set of practices and normative elements that serve to promote the common interests of a society by engendering order (and therefore constituting an international society). There are numerous interpretations of these institutions (c.f. Bull 1977; Buzan 2004). For the purposes of this analysis, a traditional approach emphasizing the role of War, the Balance of Power, Diplomacy, International Law, and Great Power Management should suffice (González-Pelaèz 2009, 103–104). These "fundamental" institutions exist in some form or another across regions and international societies and may exhibit unique qualities. Nevertheless, the current global international society is an offshoot of the European international society. It has served not only to ensure the orderly conduct of relations among European states, but also to curb the rise of revolutionary movements and other threatening states from becoming hegemonic. An international society ensures the independence and survival of its constituent states (Armstrong 1993, 1–5). The sine qua non for order and a properly functioning international society are therefore a common vision of order, a recognition by member states of their common interest, relative interstate peace, and stability in property rights. In this respect, the phenomenon of how states perceive and articulate security threats is of paramount importance. The idea of raison de système is a central tenant of early-modern European statecraft and in some ways a prerequisite to a balance of power. A modern rendition of the idea might possibly be explored as a form of macrosecuritisation (Buzan and Wæver 2009, 254). For a discussion of the merits of applying the idea to the Middle East, see (Malmvig, 145–148). Achieving order would necessitate a commonly held referent of, and consensus on, what constitutes a threat to the common interests of the members of an international society. Failure to obtain a common vision may compel regional states to pursue alliances with extra-regional powers or tempt them to project power through non-state actors.

The requirement for a common vision, as well as states' recognition of each other's common interests, is problematic in view of the imperial means by which European society came to encompass the globe. This problem is further compounded by the political and cultural diversity of international politics, which calls into question the popular notion that the international system and international society are uniform and all-encompassing arenas (c.f. Buzan and Wæver; Hurrell 2007; Costa-Buranelli 2015). Be they coercive or cooperative, interactions are denser within regions where independent political units share greater cultural and historical affinities, which can act as the wellspring of an international society (González-Pelaèz 2009, 114–115). Buzan notes that eggs on a frying pan serves as a better analogy for international society, as the "global egg white" represents the *sine qua non* values of European international society, while the "yolks" represent the dense set of interactions and *sui generis* values of individual regions (Buzan 2004, 208). From such a perspective, a Middle Eastern society is unproblematic, especially for Buzan, who characterizes the Middle East as a subglobal society of states with its own distinct character (Buzan 2009, 240). Nevertheless, he qualifies this statement by recognizing the possibility of significant heterogeneity (Buzan 2009; Buzan and Wæver 2003). For a "region" like the Middle East, heir to a centuries old legacy of external great power interventions, externally imposed regime changes, religious conflict, and lack of a unifying regional vision, there is no "yolk." For all intents and purposes, the present chapter finds greater utility in thinking about regional international societies like the Middle East as being "lightly scrambled eggs", in which an amorphous yolk is connected to the yolks of other regional international societies by way of extra-regional great powers' involvement.

This chapter therefore explores the extent to which such logic obtains in the contemporary Middle East. To what extent do states act purposively with the view of promoting each other's common interests — the raison de système — of Middle Eastern international society, and to what extent are the region's dysfunctions insurmountable? Rather than analyzing the region from a structural English school framework that highlights the functioning of "primary", "derivative", and "secondary" institutions of international society, this chapter attempts the modest goal of clarifying some of the obstacles to the consolidation of a stronger international society in the Middle East by delving into notable problems at the global, regional, state, and sub-state levels, as well as exploring the consequences of these issues for regional order. Although it may seem impertinent to attempt to disaggregate these dynamics since they are often multi-causal and mutually reinforcing, the table below advances a useful starting point that forms the core of the present theoretical investigation.

Level of Analysis	Issue	Consequence for Regional Practices
Global	• Great-power interference	• Great power co-option of regional states
Regional	• Anti-hegemonic attitudes	• Bandwagoning with extra-regional powers
State	• State weakness	• Legitimacy problems and regime insecurity
Sub-State	• Non-state/Illicit actors	• Incentives for proxy wars • Illicit economy • Civil war • Refugees

Table 1. A summary of the intersection of issues and their regional consequences on the regional raison de système.

Global Level

The first challenge to the establishment of order in the Middle East originates from outside of the region itself, through the medium of great power intervention. This is a well-documented and perennial feature of the politics of the region that continues to create deep fault lines among its constitutive members (Halliday 2009, 6). The Middle East is a region that has frequently experienced foreign occupation and forcible regime changes, going as far back as a millennium. In fact, few homegrown regional powers have emerged in the region after the Rashidun Caliphate and its successors. Where truly powerful states emerged, their interests transcended the arbitrary geographic and political boundaries of the "Middle East". Various iterations of Mongolian and Turkish conquerors over time prevented the development of a regional consciousness independent of the broader designs of empire builders with ecumenical ambitions extending far beyond the Middle East. Until very recently, there were no "political units" so to speak that could conceive of a separate Middle Eastern region with its own distinct logic. The very term "Middle East" was neither an administrative unit of the Sublime Porte, nor some eschatological goal for aspirants of liberty. It is as external an imposition as were many of the Westphalian values imposed on the region after the dismantling of the Ottoman Empire. The concept ironically originates from the reflections of Mahan (1902), a naval strategist from a rising world power, although epithets for the region abound (Davidson 1960).

The contemporary territorial division of the region is the result of external great power intervention, as evidenced by the patterns of state formation, state society dynamics, and the trajectories of regimes. During the Cold War, superpower competition in the region, external interventions, and alliance dynamics also served to weaken regional solidarity. The unconditional support of the US to Israel and Saudi Arabia, the Western backed coup in Iran and the eventual revolution in 1979, and political instability are revealing examples. This trend in regional security dynamics persists in the post-Cold War era as well, most notably with the successive interventions against Iraq. The First Gulf War highlights the absence of an intraregional sense of a balance of power, and the inability of Middle-Eastern states and organizations to moderate the behavior of one of its members. To ensure regional peace, Middle Eastern states deferred to a resurgent United States, which resolved the conflict through a UN-sanctioned intervention. The US-led preemptive war against Iraq in 2003 is even more controversial as it demonstrated the vulnerability of the Middle East to external intervention, as well as how extra-regional powers can use force to reengineer the region by forcibly imposing regime change.

Since the publication of *International Society and the Middle East* in 2009, several regimes in the region have been contested, which has drawn considerable attention and interference from great powers and states aspiring to regional leadership. The most significant of these cases is the ongoing Syrian Civil War. This conflict, in many respects resulting from the financial and material support of regional powers to various factions within and beyond Syria, features an authoritarian and purportedly secular regime in Syria, backed by Russia and Iran, versus a hodgepodge of internally divided Sunni factions backed by Gulf Monarchies and Turkey, Kurdish groups favored by the West, and ISIS. More importantly, the human rights abuses, the alleged use of chemical weapons, and the region's incapacity (with some exceptions) to provide humanitarian assistance for refugees underscore the fundamental fragility of regional international society. These contemporary developments are important because they evidence a general lack of common vision for the region, as well as the failure of Middle Eastern states to act towards a *raison de système*. Instead, prominent Middle Eastern states have pursued ineffective foreign policies based on parochial conceptualizations of order; these are explored in the next section.

Regional Level

Related to the external factors above, another obstacle to the emergence of a common vision of order is that there are no great powers within the Middle East that can effectively bring to bear sufficient political influence and material capabilities to sway other states and thereby "manage" the region's international relations. One partial explanation for the absence of Middle Eastern great powers is the region's colonial history and the strong anti-hegemonic tendencies of Middle Eastern states *inter se*, as they prefer to balance with external powers against regional rivals. This may appear as a controversial point. After all, while some historical international societies coalesced around hegemonic systems (like that of the Sino-centric international society), the European international society developed in an "anarchical" setting (Kaufmann, Little, and Wohlforth 2007, 234; Watson 1990; Bull and Watson 1985; Bull 1977). However, great powers still played a decisive role in shaping their international society through peace settlements and fulfilling a "concert" function (Bull 1977, 194–222).

In the European context, great powers allowed an element of hierarchy and, by some accounts, exercised a collective hegemony that effectively helped preserve a peaceful order (Clark 2011). The Concert of Europe, while repressive in many violent ways, was successful in moderating great-power wars and revolutionary social movements that could harm the fabric of international society. There were also great powers external to the core of European international society that could enervate such developments in meaningful ways. When the European situation is contrasted to that of the Middle East, the latter remains too politically diverse to accommodate a "thicker" international society, while also lacking intra-regional great powers to collectively articulate regional interests and collaborate on achieving them. It must, however, be said that one notable vision, that of Pan-Arabism, fell apart due to an unsuccessful bid for regional leadership.

The most notable of these might have been the cases of Nasser and Sadat in Egypt and Saddam Hussain in Iraq. Although these bids were also alternatingly supported or resisted to some extent by local powers, some progress was made towards a Middle Eastern great power through the unification of Egypt and Syria, which formed the Great Arab Republic between 1958–1961. Nevertheless, this could not be sustained without further unity and political support by other relevant states. Their failure to resolve the Israeli–Palestinian conflict combined with Egypt's eventual normalization of relations with Israel not only dashed hopes but also undermined Egypt's bid for the leadership of the Arab world. In the post-Cold War, Saddam's efforts to pursue the cause of Arab states, which (he thought) entitled his state to the occupation of Kuwait, was frustrated by the Gulf War coalition led by the United States.

Not only did Pan-Arabism fail to bring unity, but the logic of the Cold War also raised Islamic identity as a popular alternative rallying idea in the face of the threat of communism. While this could have served as a much more inclusive identity, possibly appealing to non-Arab and nominally secular countries as well, culture acted as a centrifugal force. This is not to suggest an essentialist perspective. The Sunni–Shia conflict is one that harkens back to the founding of Islam in the 7th century and therefore understandably cuts across many regional cleavages. However, power and diverging interests are the root of this conflict. It is a clear manifestation of the underlying competition between US-supported "Petromonarchies" and Israel versus Iran and its proxies. Contributing to this was the successful securitization of Iran and Syria. Iran's nuclear program, whether genuinely peaceful or "roguish," was sufficiently threatening to its neighbors to preclude cooperation on several issues (Kaye and Wehrey 2007).

The most recent but ineffective bid for regional leadership came from Turkey under its *zero problems with neighbors* policy. Inspired by Ahmet Davutoğlu's *Strategic Depth* doctrine, Turkey embarked on a regional peace building policy couched in the language of liberal humanitarianism and soft power projection, which has received much criticism (Özkan 2014). Yet, this policy failed to gain sufficient international traction and succeeded only in causing a diplomatic crisis between Israel and Turkey. This was useful for Turkey's domestic political purposes, but disagreements precluded the possibility of effective inter-state collaboration in alleviating the suffering of Palestinians (the original justification of the diplomatic incidence) and in allowing the latter government to conduct populism on "Arab Street." None of these movements proved to be successful or provided the kind of impetus to advance a regional international society in the same way as the Treaty of Utrecht or the Congress of Vienna did for the European case.

State Level

The previous section highlighted the lack of a common vision for the Middle East and pointed out numerous bids for the privilege of articulating the interests of a Middle Eastern international society. Now a far more fundamental problem needs to be addressed; a point that also helps to explain the absence of regional great powers as well. Middle Eastern regimes are comparatively weaker than their counterparts elsewhere. The absence of a history of independent statehood, the lack of correspondence between borders and confessional preferences, and the unavailability of traditional state-building venues to Middle Eastern states have traditionally prevented the consolidation of most states (Jackson and James 1993). English school scholars often point out that it is worth studying European international society because its constituent members successfully spread overseas to assimilate otherwise disparate and isolated international societies formed around distant civilization cores (Buzan 2001, 484). This bloody and contested process eventually allowed European norms and practices, albeit with local variations, to shape aspects of other regional international societies, thereby helping to integrate them with the rest of the globe. What propelled European great powers to "success" was a combination of events, but most notably a competitive geopolitical environment that was favorable, especially in the nascent period of European international society, to war making and state-building (Tilly 1992, 1–3). War allowed powerful sovereigns to conquer territories, acquire wealth, build administrative and extractive capabilities, incorporate social classes into the state apparatus, and create unifying national ideas all the while extinguishing less effective and cohesive units (Tilly 1992, 24–25). Despite its long history of European-style war making, the sheer scale and organizational logic of the Ottoman Empire precluded the possibility of an effective, centralized imperial administration. Various Middle Eastern states had the opportunity to emulate the successes of European state-builders, but were eventually rebuked by external intervention (Lustick 1997). The only comparably cohesive states appear to be the ones that were former imperial powers themselves, or which successfully mobilized popular support against foreign occupation.

The state formation and consequent state transformation trajectory of Middle Eastern states also served to limit intraregional cooperation by creating inward-looking insecure regimes. This is an interesting counterpoint to regions like Latin America where states have also remained institutionally weak, and intra-state violence high due to the interests of regimes; but unlike the Middle East, inter-state peace and cooperation is remarkably robust (Centeno 2003; Martín 2006). Simply put, the antagonisms in state-society relations have led to regime insecurity in these states, therefore resulting in internally oriented security apparati (viz. Andreski 1980, 3–10; Ayoob 1996;

Jackson 1990; David 1991; Barnett and Levy1991; Holsti 1996; Lustick 1997). One can posit, especially in the context of the Cold War, that conducting alliance politics with the view of defeating internal dissent and mobilizing public support for the regime was a higher security priority than making concessions in favor of a *raison de système*. However, this may not necessarily present an obstacle to the operation of an international society, because similar dynamics were in operation in European international society and arguably in Latin America's international society as well. In the case of the former, in the 19th century, the Concert of Europe, comprised of reactionary monarchies that repressed progressive forces within European states, is a perfect example: a system established with the view of providing security to insecure states. Similarly, as in the case of Operation Cóndor Latin America provided political asylum to ostracized political leaders and their military establishments, also facilitated by the US, and often cooperated with each other to carry out domestic repression against threats to their regimes (Martín 2006, 167). Such solidarity has been absent in the Middle East as states have frequently aided violent non-state actors to undermine each other. An examination of sub-state actors in the Middle East may help reveal why such "solidarity" failed to manifest among Middle Eastern states even when some states faced challenges from similar sources, or of a similar kind.

Sub-State Level

The final implication for "order-weakness" in the Middle East is with regard to non-state actors. The divisions within Middle Eastern states and perennial state-weakness add layers of complexity, as international societies are less likely to thrive in the absence of sufficiently stable states capable of providing domestic order. The failure of the Middle East to establish regional order provides non-state actors with opportunities to pursue diverse and conflictive agendas that undermine regional international society. But before discussing non-state actors in the region, it may be useful to note that the English school traditionally advocates the functioning of international law and the "sacred" quality of sovereignty (Bull 1966; Jackson 1990). Respect for sovereignty, a recognition of the differences in the politics and aspirations of states in the pursuit of international order, is what makes an "anarchical society" possible. The classical, "pluralist," understanding of international society argues for a stronger sense of non-intervention in the domestic affairs of states.

The English school also embraces the idea of humanity as being an inseparable part of "world society," in which individuals and groups of states are the main referents, and notions of shared values and recognition of the broader interests of humanity are more important than states. "Solidarism" refers to a global fraternity of humanity that denounces efforts by states to impose order using force, and argues for the potential necessity of violating sovereignty for promoting normative ends such as justice and humanitarian causes. Of course, where an asymmetry of power is unavoidable, principles are usually abused. Powerful members of international society often set demanding expectations on its peripheral members and justify punishing them (Gong 1984; Stroikos 2014).

How do these concepts apply in the case of the Middle East? Non-state actors can, on the one hand, embody the normative aspirations of a regional international society and possibly the broader global world society. Many of these movements, for example the PKK, Hamas, and Hezbollah purport to pursue justice, either by acting on the right to self-determination, or as resistance against oppressors but are also considered to be terrorist actors by most states. Yet, they can also undermine international society because they challenge the basis for collective action by exacerbating regime insecurity, or simply by undermining functioning states. Without condoning violations of human rights, it must be said that great powers and regional powers alike have a proclivity towards justifying their interventions on lofty discourses of human rights. The First and Second Gulf Wars highlighted humanitarian sentiments in addition to broader global security concerns. Humanitarian concerns also animated the discussions concerning the 2011 intervention in Libya, and more recently, the debates surrounding Syria. In addition to being used for justifying interventions, non-state actors can become instruments of statecraft, as many have frequently been utilized as proxies by other regional and global powers to promote political and even economic goals. Iran's role in supporting Hezbullah and Hafez Assad's support for the PKK in the 1990s are example of how non-state actors can be used for power projection (Kirschner 2016).

The persistence of powerful non-state actors, violent or not, can undermine regional international society by incentivizing external and regional powers to act in self-regarding ways, which is ultimately detrimental to the regional society's interests. This is not some unique dysfunction of Middle Eastern international society either, for non-state actors have historically operated either independently within international society or have been used as instruments of coercive statecraft to promote the *raison d'état* of states (Thompson 1996).

Some of the most important security challenges at the non-state level since the publication of *International Society and the Middle East* include state weakness in Iraq, economic and societal problems in the broader region instigating the "Arab Spring" and a Civil War in Syria, and most importantly, the emergence of ISIS. ISIS is a product of many of the cross-cutting problems in the Middle East and presents yet another challenge to regional order not only in terms of its contestation of established states and the overtly violent means with which it pursues its goals, but also its manifestation of the lack of a unifying and policy moderating vision of order in Middle Eastern international society.

ISIS operates, in many ways, just like the purveyors of private violence pursuing policies akin to state-builders, as was the case in early modern European history. For example, ISIS's earlier activities in Iraq were likened by some to a "blitzkrieg" as ISIS fought across Iraqi territory and, like modern day privateers, looted the city of Mosul in summer 2014, including a branch of the Iraqi Central Bank. In other places of the world, such an audacious and effective operation by illicit entrepreneurs (terrorist or otherwise) would be unthinkable. The most interesting of ISIS's functions pertain to its creation of economic networks to smuggle illicit goods as well as critical strategic resources such as oil. For countries with low resource endowments, the prospects of accessing oil well below market prices is too good an opportunity to pass up. In the case of ISIS, the methods are straightforward and low-tech. Once oil is extracted from wells and refined in boot-leg refineries, it could be disseminated for cheap domestic consumption (thanks to makeshift pipelines, among other means), or to the world market through "legitimate" actors (Giovanni *et al.* 2014). In the case of Syria, there already was such a precedent, as much of its comparatively meagre oil production was used to (legally and illegally) procure foreign currency, even before the civil war. Previously, ISIS controlled oil fields in Northern Syria and Northern Iraq, and could sell oil below market prices through collusion with the governments in the region. Furthermore, the consumers include local sellers as well as representatives of oil companies (al-Khatteeb 2014). Interestingly, the smuggling activities were shared by many factions, including ones that ISIS is fighting against such as the Kurds, the Baghdad government, the Assad regime, and Turkey (Cohen 2014).

In this context, it may also sound unfair to suggest that such apparent dysfunctions are undermining Middle Eastern international society. There are, of course, reasons to believe that non-state violence should not be regarded as detrimental to international order *per se*. As the history of European international society and the eventual pacification of Mediterranean privateering attests, instability and uncertainty often help states to see the proverbial bigger picture (Colás 2016). The need of European powers to regulate private violence aided in the development of laws and practices, all of which ultimately contributed to the consolidation of European states, and therefore European international society (Thompson 1996, 3, 9; Colás 2016, 85). Despite the short-term interests of states and acts of collusion between states and ISIS during this conflict, there appears to be a general consensus among the great powers and regional states that ISIS is a threat to the regional order, even if earnest efforts against it have been slow to materialize.

A last point of concern in Middle Eastern international society is that of tragedies, such as the ongoing Syrian refugee crisis, which has forced over 11 million Syrians to flee their country since the beginning of the war. In a conflict that could have been mitigated at its onset, had it not been for the attitudes of powers interested in changing the Syrian regime, the heavy humanitarian toll could have been averted. However, the attempts by states to alleviate the crisis also merit guarded optimism not only about Middle Eastern international society, but also the global international society. Most notably, the countries neighboring Syria host nearly five million of these refugees, with Lebanon, Turkey, and Jordan being the most active in this regard. Many others have been accepted by Western countries despite vituperative domestic debates. These efforts may be inadequate even with financial aid from regional and extra-regional powers, but it also shows the resilience of at least a modicum of humanitarian sentiments that is the cornerstone of any social or international order, be it a pluralist or solidarist one.

Conclusion

In attempting to discuss order and international society in the Middle East, this chapter has depicted a decidedly ambivalent picture. The number of extra-regional challenges and disunity among and within its constituent states, as well as a plethora of intra-regional challenges from violent non-state actors, cast doubts about the efficacy of Middle Eastern international society in delivering a tenable regional order. It is still in a state of flux in which power politics and threats confine the loci of states' security interests to within their borders, and this further hampers the effective functioning of a regional society. In spite of this, historical precedence and some contemporary developments in tackling common threats and attempting to uphold normative practices also point to the indelible influence of a global international society and its humanitarian sentiments in moderating the collateral damage of unbound *raison d'état* behavior.

References

Al-Khatteeb, Luay. 2014. "How Iraq's black market in oil funds ISIS," *CNN* (August 22, 2014). Last Modified: October 20, 2017. http://edition.cnn.com/2014/08/18/business/al-khatteeb-isis-oil-iraq/.

Andreski, Stanislav. 1980. "On the Peaceful Disposition of Dictatorships," *Journal of Strategic Studies* 3, no. 3 (January): 3–10.

Armstrong, David. 1993. *Revolution and World Order: The Revolutionary State in International Society.* Oxford: Oxford University Press.

Ayoob, Muhammed. 1996. "State-Making, State-Breaking and State Failure: Explaining the Roots of 'Third World' Insecurity." In *Between Development and Destruction: An Enquiry into the Causes of Conflict in Post-Colonial States* edited by Luc van de Goor, Kumar Rupesinghe, and Paul Sciarone, 67–90. London: Palgrave Macmillan.

Bagge, Carsten and Ole Wæver, "In Defense of Religion: Sacred Referents of Securitization," *Millennium: Journal of International Studies* 29, no. 3 (2000): 705–739.

Barnett, Michael N. and Jack S. Levy. 1991. "Domestic Sources of Alliances and Alignments: The Case of Egypt, 1962–1973." *International Organization* 45, No. 3 (Summer): 369–395.

Black, Ian et al. 2016. "The Terrifying rise of Isis: $2bn in loot, online killings and an army on the run," *The Guardian* (June 16, 2014). Last modified: November 20, 2016. http://www.theguardian.com/world/2014/jun/16/terrifying-rise-of-isis-iraq-executions

Bull, Hedley. 1966. "The Grotian Conception of International Society." In *Diplomatic Investigations: Essays in the Theory of International Politics,* edited by Herbert Butterfield and Martin Wight, 51–73. Cambridge, MA: Harvard University Press.

Bull, Hedley. 1977. *The Anarchical Society: A Study of Order in World Politics.* New York, NY: Columbia University Press.

Buzan, Barry. 2001. "The English School: An Underexploited Resource." *Review of International Studies* 27, no. 3 (July): 471–488. https://doi.org/10.1017/S026021050100471.

Buzan, Barry and Ole Wæver. 2003. *Regions and Power: The Structure of International Security*. Cambridge: Cambridge University Press.

Buzan, Barry. 2004. *From International to World Society.* Cambridge: Cambridge University Press.

Buzan, Barry and Ole Wæver. 2009. "Macrosecuritisation and Security Constellations: Reconsidering Scale in Securitisation." *Review of International Studies* 35 (April): 253–276.

Centeno, Miguel A. 2003. *Blood and Debt: War and the Nation-State in Latin America*. Penn State Press.

Clark, Ian. 2011. *Hegemony in International Society.* Oxford: Oxford University Press.

Cohen, David. 2014. "Remarks of Under Secretary for Terrorism and Financial Intelligence David S. Cohen at The Carnegie Endowment for International Peace, Attacking ISIS's Financial Foundation," *US Department of the Treasury* (October 23, 2014): http://kyleorton1991.wordpress.com/2014/03/24/assessing-the-evidence-of-collusion-between-the-assad-regime-and-the-wahhabi-jihadists-part-1/

Colas, Alejandro. 2016. "Barbary Coast in the Expansion of International Society: Piracy, Privateering, and Corsairing as Primary Institutions, *Review of International Studies,* 42, no. 5 (December): 840–857.

Costa-Buranelli, Filippo. 2015. "'Do you know what I mean?' 'Not Exactly': English School, Global International Society, and the Polsemy of Institutions," *Global Discourse,* 5, no. 3 (July): 499–514.

David, Stephen R. 1991. "Explaining Third-World Alignment," *World Politics,* 43, no. 2 (January): 233–256.

Davison, Roderick H. 1960. "Where is the Middle East?" *International Affairs,* 38, No. 4 (July): 665–675.

Giovanni, Janine di, Leah McGrath Goodman, and Damien Sharkov. 2014 "How Does ISIS Fund Its Reign of Terror?" *Newsweek* (October 6). *Last modified April 20, 2017.* http://www.newsweek.com/2014/11/14/how-does-isis-fund-its-reign-terror-282607.html.

Gong, Gerrit. 1984. *The Standard of 'Civilisation' in International Society*. Oxford: Clarendon Press.

González-Pelaèz, Ana. 2009. "The Primary Institutions of Middle Eastern International Society." In *International Society and the Middle East: English*

School Theory at the Regional Level edited by Barry Buzan and Ana González-Pelaèz, 92–117. New York, NY: Palgrave Macmillan.

Halliday, Fred. 2009. "The Middle East and Conceptions of 'International Society.'" In *International Society and the Middle East,* edited by Barry Buzan and González-Pelaèz, 1–23, New York, NY: Palgrave Macmillan.

Holsti, Kalevi J. 1996. *The State, War, and the State of War.* Cambridge: Cambridge University Press.

Hurrell, Andrew. 2007. *On Global Order: Power, Values, and the Constitution of International Society.* Oxford: Oxford University Press.

Jackson, Robert H. 2000. *The Global Covenant: Human Conduct in a World of States*. Oxford: Oxford University Press.

Jackson, Robert H. 1990. *Quasi-States: Sovereignty, International Relations and the Third World.* Cambridge: Cambridge University Press.

Jackson, Robert H. and Alan James. 1993. *States in a Changing World: A Contemporary Analysis* Oxford: Claredon Press.

Kaufmann, Stuart, Richard Little, and William. C. Wohlforth. 2007. *The Balance of Power in World History.* New York, NY: Palgrave Macmillan.

Kaye, Dalia Dassa and Frederic M. Wehrey. 2007. "A Nuclear Iran: The Reactions of Neighbours," *Survival: Global Politics and Strategy,* 49, no. 2 (June): 111–128.

Kirchner, Magdelena. 2016. *Why States Rebel: Understanding State Sponsorship of Terrorism*. Opladen: Barbara Budrich Publishers.

Lustick, Robert. 1997. "The Absence of Middle Eastern Great Powers: Political 'Backwardness' in Historical Perspective." *International Organization,* 51, no. 4 (Autumn): 653–683.

Mahan, Alfred T. 1902. *The Persian Gulf and International Relations*. London: Robert Theobald.

Malmvig, Helle. 2014. "Power, Identity and Securitisation in the Middle East: Regional after the Arab Uprisings," *Mediterranean Politics,* 19, no. 1 (December): 145–148.

Martín, Felix E. 2006. *The Militarist Peace: Conditions for War and Peace.* New York, NY: Palgrave Macmillan.

Özkan, Behlul. 2014. "Davutoglu and the Idea of Pan-Islamism." *Survival,* 57 (July): 63–84.

Stroikos, Dimitrios. 2014. "Introduction: Rethinking the Standard(s) of Civilisation(s) in International Relations." *Millennium: Journal of International Studies,* 42, No. 3 (August): 546–556.

Thompson, Janice E. 1996. *Mercenaries, Pirates, and Sovereigns: State-Building and Extra-Territorial Violence in Early Modern Europe.* Princeton, NJ: Princeton University Press.

Tilly, Charles. 1992. *Coercion and Capital: State-Formation in European History 990–1992.* Blackwell.

Watson, Adam. 1990. "Systems of States," *Review of International Studies* 16 (April): 99–109.

3

United States Foreign Policy in the Middle East after the Cold War

JONATHAN CRISTOL

On 2 August 1990, the people of Kuwait City awoke at 5am to the sound of Iraqi tanks rolling down their streets. Iraqi President Saddam Hussein intended to annex the small Sheikhdom of Kuwait, Iraq's "19th province," and tap its massive oil reserves. The invasion did not come entirely out of nowhere. Iraqi troops were massed at the border as the result of an oil dispute with its tiny neighbor, and the United States tried to persuade Iraq to solve its problems with Kuwait peacefully. This action was the first time one sovereign state had invaded and annexed another since Indonesia annexed East Timor in 1975; and it was the first major challenge to world order since the 1989 fall of the Berlin Wall. This chapter examines key events in US foreign policy in the Middle East from Saddam Hussein's invasion of Iraq in 1990 to Donald Trump's announcement of US withdrawal from the Iran nuclear deal in 2018. It shows how America's strong position at the end of the Cold War and the end of Operation Desert Storm in 1991 led to a period of American hyperinvolvement in Middle Eastern politics that ultimately weakened its regional standing.

The Persian Gulf War

The global reaction to Saddam Hussein's invasion and annexation of Kuwait was virtually universally negative. The United Nations Security Council (UNSC) issued Resolution 660, demanding that "Iraq withdraw immediately and unconditionally all its forces to the positions in which they were located on 1 August 1990." Saddam Hussein's blatant act of aggression and territorial aggrandizement put an end to decades of stalemate in the Security Council when the USSR and the US voted together on UNSCR 660.

It was not immediately obvious how the United States would react to Saddam's aggression; and it was by no means certain that the US had any interest in fighting a war to restore Kuwait's sovereignty. Congress was divided. The Senate approved the use of force against Iraq by a vote of just 52–47, significantly closer than the 77–23 approval of the 2003 Iraq War. President George H.W. Bush saw an opportunity to establish a "new world order" in which territorial aggrandizement was a product of the past, and adherence to global norms was the wave of the future. He supported a war and it was his decision to make.

Bush wanted a grand coalition operating with UN approval, not a purely American intervention. UNSCR 678 passed on 29 November 1990. It gave Saddam Hussein "one final opportunity" to withdraw from Kuwait. If he did not, the resolution, "Authorize[d] Member States… to use all necessary means" to compel him. "Operation Desert Storm" began on 17 January 1991. Nearly every country in the world joined the coalition – Yemen backed Iraq and Jordan remained neutral. Americans fought alongside 31 diverse countries' armed forces. Saudi Arabia, Kuwait, United Arab Emirates, Japan, South Korea, and Germany were the major funders of the war effort. In the end, the US Congress's General Accountability Office found that Desert Shield and Desert Storm were, "fully financed from allied contributions without using US taxpayer funds" (Conahan 1991, 12). The Warsaw Pact did not provide support, but it did not interfere. The zero-sum world had ended, and the Warsaw Pact dissolved itself on 1 July 1991.

Desert Storm ended on 28 February 1991. Saddam Hussein was still president on 1 March. President Bush and Brent Scowcroft, Bush's national security advisor, said of the decision not to remove Saddam Hussein from power, "Trying to eliminate Saddam, extending the ground war into an occupation of Iraq, would have violated our guideline about not changing objectives in midstream… and would have incurred incalculable human and political costs… We would have been forced to occupy Baghdad and, in effect, rule Iraq… Had we gone the invasion route, the US could conceivably still be an occupying power in a bitterly hostile land" ("Bush on Iraq" 1998, par. 3). The world would later learn just how accurate that assessment was.

The defeat of Saddam Hussein is often described as the peak of American power and global influence. One headline called it, "the pinnacle of American military supremacy" (Blair 2016). It resulted in the establishment of new American bases in Bahrain, Kuwait, Qatar, and Saudi Arabia (bases that were soon used to establish "no fly" zones to protect Iraq's Kurdish and Shia populations), and record personal popularity for President Bush. Bush decided to use the high standing of the United States, and his personal popularity, to bring an end to the Israeli/Arab conflict.

Israel and the Peace Process

United States support for Israel has been a consistent feature of US foreign policy in the Middle East for more than 40 years. The US/Israel relationship is often portrayed as unwavering, but there are periods of tension and stark disagreements.

In Desert Storm, President Bush asked Israeli President Yitzhak Shamir not to retaliate in the event of an Iraqi attack. It was more than just a polite request. Secretary of Defense Dick Cheney refused Israel's request for the "friend/foe" codes that would allow its fighters to identity enemy aircraft. This made it effectively impossible for Israeli fighters to engage Iraqi targets without risking the accidental downing of a friendly plane. In recompense, the US deployed its Patriot missile defense system to protect Israeli cities from Saddam Hussein's Scud missile attacks. The missile impacts caused two deaths and injured over 1,000 (Haberman 1995, par. 7). Despite early reports heralding the Patriots' success, a 1991 Israeli Air Force report concluded, "there is no evidence of even a single successful intercept" (Weiner 1993, par. 5). Nevertheless, American pressure kept Israel out of the conflict.

Secretary of State James Baker arranged a conference in Madrid on 30 October – 4 November 1991. The participants were the US, USSR, Israel, Syria, Lebanon, Jordan, and representatives of the Palestinians on the West Bank and in Gaza. This was the first time that these parties sat together, and one of the last times that the USSR sat with anybody. The Soviet Union formally dissolved on 26 December 1991.

The Madrid Conference did not itself yield any significant achievements, but led to the mutual recognition between Israel and the Palestine Liberation Organization (PLO), which was not present in Madrid. It also set in motion secret talks between Israel and the PLO in Oslo, Norway. These talks led to framework agreements on Israeli–Palestinian peace – Oslo 1 and Oslo 2 (the "Oslo Accords"). But the George H.W. Bush Administration would not be a part of further negotiations. Bill Clinton defeated Bush in the 1992 election and made Israeli–Palestinian peace a presidential priority.

Nine months after Clinton's inauguration, PLO Chairman Yasser Arafat and Israeli Prime Minister Yitzhak Rabin shook hands with Clinton and with each other on the White House lawn. The Oslo Accords had been negotiated largely without American help, but Oslo was a "process" and the two parties were just at the start. The premise of the Oslo Process was the "two-state solution" as the basis for a final Israeli–Palestinian peace agreement. Arafat returned from his Tunisian exile to the West Bank to assume control of the new "Palestinian Authority" (PA).

The Oslo Accords did not discuss four major issues, which were deemed "final status issues" to be resolved at an indeterminate later date. These issues were: the status of Jerusalem; final borders; the fate of Israeli settlements; and the fate of Palestinian refugees. President Clinton played an active role in the negotiations between Israel and the PA, but the hopes expressed that day on the White House lawn did not last long. Rabin's assassination by a Jewish extremist on 4 November 1995 and a wave of suicide bombings by the Hamas terrorist group were just two factors that caused the "peace process" to stall.

Clinton brought Arafat and Israeli Prime Minister Ehud Barak to Camp David for two weeks in Summer 2000. The two sides came closer than ever before to reaching an agreement. After Camp David, President Clinton developed his own peace proposal. The day after George W. Bush's inauguration the two sides met again in Taba, Egypt in an attempt to reach a final agreement based on Clinton's proposal. However, the negotiations at Taba were cut short by Israel's election of Ariel Sharon as its new prime minister. He had a different view of the peace process, and the same four issues remain between them today.

Osama bin Laden and al-Qaeda

The Israeli/Palestinian peace process was just one of many major events that followed Desert Storm. The Saudi royal family may have been grateful to America for protecting the Kingdom, but not everyone was happy about a permanent American presence so close to Mecca and Medina. It was a particular affront to Osama bin Laden. Bin Laden fought in Afghanistan against the Soviet Union, and there he met a man named Abdullah Azzam. Together they founded al-Qaeda, "The Base," in 1988. Al-Qaeda was quickly linked to a series of terrorist acts against the US including a 26 February 1993 attack on the World Trade Center and the 25 June 1996 attack on the US military installation in Dhahran, Saudi Arabia.

US intelligence agencies were keenly aware of bin Laden and attuned to the danger he presented, but he was not yet a household name. Bin Laden made international news on 7 August 1998 when al-Qaeda suicide terrorists blew up the US embassies in Kenya and Tanzania. In retaliation the US launched cruise missiles against an alleged al-Qaeda chemical weapons facility in Sudan and against al-Qaeda training camps in Khost, Afghanistan. As it turned out, the alleged chemical weapons facility was a pharmaceutical firm and the strike was widely criticized.

Bin Laden was not deterred by the US missile strikes. On 12 October 2000, al-Qaeda forces drove a small boat up to the USS Cole, a naval frigate docked in Aden, Yemen, and detonated an explosive device. 17 sailors were killed. The lead FBI investigator of the attack was Special Agent John O'Neil, who would be one of 3,000 people murdered by al-Qaeda on 11 September 2001.

On the morning of "9/11," 19 hijackers boarded planes with the intent of hijacking them. Airplane hijackings had been a regular tactic of terrorist groups for decades, but al-Qaeda introduced a new innovation. Rather than use the hijackings to make demands and extract concessions, they used them as the world's largest suicide bombs.

The hijackers crashed two into the World Trade Center, collapsing both buildings and a neighboring building. They crashed one into the Pentagon, and, realizing what was going on, the passengers on the fourth took control and crashed United Flight 93 into an empty field. Osama bin Laden had made good on his 23 February 1998 fatwa, "The ruling to kill the Americans and their allies—civilians and military—is an individual duty for every Muslim who can do it in any country in which it is possible to do it." The United States reaction was not swift, but it was severe.

Three days later, on 14 September 2001, Bush received from Congress an "Authorization for the Use of Military Force" (AUMF), which authorized him "to use all necessary and appropriate force" not only against those responsible for the 9/11 attacks, but also "in order to prevent any future acts of international terrorism against the United States." This vague and ill-defined authorization has since been used to justify US deployments at least 37 times in locations including Djibouti, Eritrea, Ethiopia, Georgia, Kenya, Philippines, Somalia, Syria, and Yemen (Weed 2006, 2). The AUMF has given three presidents broad powers, but it was originally written to authorize the invasion of Afghanistan and the pursuit of Osama bin Laden and al-Qaeda.

The United States knew immediately that Osama bin Laden was behind 9/11 and gave the Taliban government of Afghanistan one final chance to turn him over to the US. They declined, and the United States invaded Afghanistan on 7 October 2001. The Taliban government fell on 17 December 2001.

The war in Afghanistan was not controversial and enjoyed bipartisan support. President George W. Bush (2001, par. 59) made clear in his speech to a joint session of Congress that, "any nation that continues to harbor or support terrorism will be regarded by the United States as a hostile regime." But while the Taliban's harboring of terrorists was beyond dispute, the Administration's case for war in Iraq was more controversial.

The Iraq War

The Administration's argument hinged on Saddam developing weapons of mass destruction (WMD). Secretary of State Colin Powell (2003, par. 15) made the case to the UN Security Council that, "the facts and Iraq's behavior show that Saddam Hussein and his regime are concealing their efforts to produce more weapons of mass destruction." He even had pictures to "prove" it, but we now know that his WMD programs had been defunct for many years. The International Atomic Energy Agency (IAEA) was correct in its assessment that Iraq had no active nuclear program. Powell now calls that speech a "great intelligence failure" and a "blot" on his record (Breslow 2016, par. 1). Nevertheless, the Bush Administration proceeded with its war planning.

Despite Powell's best efforts, the UNSC declined to authorize the use of force. In contrast to his father's global coalition, Bush proceeded with a "Coalition of the Willing" made up largely of the United States, United Kingdom, Poland, and Australia. The Coalition launched airstrikes and a ground invasion on 20 March 2003, and found Saddam Hussein hiding in a hole in the ground. The war was won easily. Saddam Hussein was not loved by his people and initially US forces were "greeted as liberators," just as Cheney had predicted (Cheney and Russert 2003, par. 4). But the fanfare was short-lived and Cheney would later be mocked for the statement.

The American coalition installed Ambassador L. Paul Bremer as Administrator of the new "Coalition Provisional Authority (CPA)." Bremer quickly disbanded the Iraqi Army and purged Iraqi society of members of Saddam Hussein's Baath Party. The 424,000 members of the Iraqi Army were critical to maintaining law and order, and were generally more interested in receiving a paycheck than in loyalty to Saddam Hussein. Because of Bremer's decision they were armed and angry, and with few job prospects in the new Iraq. The situation was similar for Baath Party members above the very lowest ranks. Bremer barred them from government, but to work in government in Saddam's Iraq, one had to be a Baath party member. Thus, the CPA effectively fired the entire government bureaucracy. Nobody could run the electrical grid. Nobody could maintain critical infrastructure. The only people with real authority were the Americans. Many former soldiers and Baath party officials joined militias, and years later, some joined the so-called Islamic State (Sly 2015, par. 5).

The CPA wrote Iraq's constitution with minimal input from Iraqis. Major positions were given to young Republican Party officials. The US military was asked to provide basic law and order but was not given the training to do so. Iraqi institutions were looted and destroyed. Making matters worse, the oil ministry was well-protected. The perception of American forces was dealt a crippling blow when, on 28 April 2004, 60 Minutes aired photographs of American soldiers torturing Iraqi prisoners at Abu Ghraib, where Saddam Hussein's regime tortured its own prisoners. These images changed the average view of the United States across Iraq.

As law and order broke down, sectarian tensions and score-settling grew. Militia groups took control of towns and sections of Baghdad. Some of these groups were supportive of the American occupation; others were bitterly opposed. The Coalition faced a growing insurgency and responded with force, which only further alienated the Iraqi people.

The Iraq War produced some winners. The Iraqi Kurds worked closely with the Americans and were able to establish *de facto* independence. At the height of the insurgency in Baghdad, when over 100 civilians were killed every day, one could take a civilian flight from Europe to a stable and secure Erbil in Iraqi Kurdistan. But there was no greater winner than America's long-time regional nemesis Iran.

The United States and Iran

On 9/11, Iran had enemies on its Eastern and Western borders. Iraq invaded Iran on 22 September 1980 and fought an eight-year war against Iran that killed over 100,000 Iranians and ended in a stalemate. The Taliban murdered nine Iranian diplomats in Mazar-e-Sharif. In 2003 neither remained in power and Iran was now bordered by the US military. This was a challenge, but it was a challenge Iran could do something about. Iran's Islamic Revolutionary Guard Corps' Quds Force set about arming and training Shia militias in Iraq. One of these militias, Asa'ib Ahl al-Haq was responsible for over 6,000 attacks on American forces between 2006–2011 (Sanchez 2016, par. 12).

Iran and the United States had been at odds since a group of Iranian revolutionaries took 52 Americans hostage at the American embassy in Tehran in November 1979. Iran has a long history of support for terrorist groups and its fast-attack craft have harassed American ships in the Persian

Gulf for decades. Iranian support for terrorism and regional aggression were major concerns of the United States, but America's greatest concern about Iran was its nuclear program.

Iran had long claimed that its nuclear program was for peaceful purposes, but few believed it. The Bush Administration tightened the economic sanctions on Iran that had been in place since 1979. President Barack Obama further increased the pressure on Iran. The Obama Administration convinced many other countries to join the sanctions regime and closed loopholes on pistachios, caviar, and Persian rugs. It also began secret talks with Tehran in Oman.

In 2003, Iran's perceived need for nuclear weapons was very real. There were 150,000 US troops to its West and 13,100 US troops to its East. The United States had just mounted a war against a country that had no WMD. By the time the 2011 Oman talks led to overt talks in Europe, Iran's geopolitical situation had changed. In 2015 there were just 3,400 US troops to its West and 9,800 US troops to its East (The Associated Press 2016). The US had war fatigue from the endless slogs in Iraq and Afghanistan. Iran also suffered under the weight of the sanctions regime. These two factors brought Iran to the negotiating table. After marathon discussions and negotiations between Iranian Minister of Foreign Affairs, Mohammad Javad Zarif, US Secretary of State John Kerry, and their Russian, Chinese, French, German, and British counterparts (the P5+1) an agreement was reached.

The Joint Comprehensive Plan of Action (JCPOA), aka "the Iran Deal," lifted UN and EU sanctions on Iran, along with US nuclear-related sanctions, in exchange for intrusive inspections of Iran's nuclear sites and limitations on Iran's nuclear technology. It seemed that the question of a nuclear Iran had been significantly delayed, if not stopped entirely.

The Arab Spring

Perhaps ironically, years earlier the Bush Administration's WMD negotiations with Libya showed that negotiations with "rogue states" could work. On 19 December 2003, the Bush Administration reached a historic agreement with Libya's eccentric dictator Colonel Muammar Gaddafi. Gaddafi agreed to abandon and destroy his WMD programs, end support for terrorism, and settle accounts relating to the 1988 bombing of Pan Am Flight 103. In exchange, the United States would end all sanctions on Libya and welcome it back into the "community of nations." Libya abided by its agreement, but years later US President Barack Obama would make a decision that contributed towards an unexpected end to the dictator's 42-year reign.

The United States has a long history of supporting friendly dictators both in the Middle East and around the world. Morocco, ruled by the Alouwite Dynasty since 1631, was first to recognize America's independence. Washington has had decades-long, close relationships with the al-Sauds, the al-Khalifas of Bahrain, the al-Saids of Oman, the al-Thanis of Qatar, the al-Sabahs of Kuwait, and the Hashemite Kingdom of Jordan.

In much of the world support for dictators was a product of the Cold War, a necessary evil in the global fight against communism. With the notable exception of support for the Shah of Iran, in the Middle East the situation was different. The aggressively secular Soviet Union was never a serious potential partner for the religious Gulf region. America's support for Arab dictators was for different reasons: assuring the free flow of oil; maintaining peace or stability with Israel; balancing against Iran; or because alternative leaders were thought to be worse. The US was unexpectedly forced to grapple with the classic American tension between the promotion of liberal values and its own self-interest when, on 17 December 2010, a Tunisian food vendor named Mohamed Bouazizi burned himself alive and set off protests around the Arab world.

The Arab Spring (or, as it is known in Iran, "The Islamic Awakening") had begun and the Obama administration had to decide if it would support the democratic aspirations of (many of) the protesters or back America's long-time allies. Protests began in Tunisia, Egypt, Libya, Syria, and Bahrain and the Administration decided against a "one-size fits all approach."

Gaddafi had no intention of holding elections. He brutally suppressed protests in the Eastern city of Benghazi, killing over 100 unarmed protesters. France and the United Kingdom took the lead in an air operation designed to protect the protesters. Reluctant to get involved in another war in the Middle East, Obama pledged air support to the operation, what one of his officials described as "leading from behind" (Lizza 2011, par. 89). On 24 April 2011 the operation targeted Gaddafi directly and struck his Tripoli home, killing his son Saif al-Arab. Months later, Gaddafi would be dragged from a ditch and beaten to death by an angry mob. Gaddafi was never a close friend of the United States, but even longtime friends were not spared by the protest movement.

Egyptian President Hosni Mubarak, in power since 1981, also cracked down on protesters. At first it appeared that the US would back its long-time friend, but on 31 January 2011 Obama sent retired diplomat Frank Wisner to tell Mubarak that Obama wanted him to step down. The Muslim Brotherhood's Mohammed Morsi narrowly won Egypt's first election in 2012. The US expressed support for Morsi, but when he started infringing on Egyptians' freedoms, the people again took to the streets. On 3 July 2013 Field Marshal Abdel Fattah el-Sisi overthrew Morsi and established a military dictatorship in Egypt. This time the US remained quiet. The democratic experiment in Egypt had failed. Obama had pushed for elections in Egypt regardless of potential consequences just as Bush had eight years earlier when, on 9 January 2005, Hamas won the first and last elections held in the Gaza Strip.

The Syrian Civil War

The contagion spreading across the Middle East reached Syria on 15 March 2011. Anti-Assad riots broke out and it looked as though Assad might be caught up in the same wave that toppled leaders in Tunisia, Libya, and Egypt; but Assad had no intention of going quietly. He benefited from both his own brutal crackdown and a highly fractured opposition. The United States had no plans to intervene directly.

However, in response to a chemical attack by Assad's forces on 21 August 2013, ten days later Obama (2013, par. 5) gave a statement, "I have decided that the United States should take military action against Syrian regime targets... I'm confident we can hold the Assad regime accountable for their use of chemical weapons, deter this kind of behavior, and degrade their capacity to carry it out." The "red line" had been established. But on 11 April 2014 the Assad regime used chemical weapons again, and the US again did nothing. It was clear that despite Assad's illegal use of chemical weapons, the Obama Administration would not intervene in Syria. Instead, it relied on an agreement negotiated by Assad ally Russian President Vladimir Putin to remove Assad's chemical weapons.

Syria was the USSR's only reliable friend in the Middle East and after the Cold War it remained a friend to Russia. Moscow's sole military outpost in the Middle East was a small supply depot and naval base located in Tartus, on the Syrian coast. The Syrian Civil War provided an ideal opportunity for Putin, who saw the power vacuum created by America's perceived withdrawal from the region. Putin intervened on behalf of Assad and took the opportunity to open a new permanent air base in Hmeimim, south-east of Latakia. And while the United States had planned to stay out of Syria, the rise of a new terrorist threat in the region drew America into Syria.

The "Islamic State"

The Islamic State of Iraq and Syria (ISIS) began as "al-Qaeda in Iraq," but was expelled from the al-Qaeda network for its brutality and for its targeting of other Muslims. It grew rapidly and took over large swaths of territory in Iraq and Syria. By the end of 2014 ISIS controlled 34,000 square miles. This base of operations and ISIS's skilled fighters and (stolen) American equipment put both America's Kurdish allies, and the American-backed government in Iraq, at risk. Additionally, a series of brutal videos of ISIS members decapitating Westerners terrified the American public. The US decided it could not stand by while ISIS caused such damage and terrorized the local population. It reinserted special forces teams and advisors to assist the Kurds and the Iraqi Army in their fight against ISIS. In Syria, where Obama had long resisted American involvement, he now committed a small number of US special forces. In 2017 the new Administration increased the US presence in Syria to 2,000.

The Trump Administration and Saudi Arabia

Previous US administrations took different approaches to Middle East policy, yet they all operated within a common set of norms and accepted practices. Donald J. Trump's presidential campaign rhetoric and his actions in office marked a stark divergence from past precedent.

On the campaign trail, Trump articulated a mix of isolationist and hyper-aggressive policies. He opposed the Iraq War, but also thought that America's biggest mistake was not taking Iraq's oil. He supported the use of torture against terrorists and called for killing terrorists' families. He questioned the long-standing relationship with Saudi Arabia. Less than two weeks into his campaign, Trump tweeted, "Saudi Arabia should be paying the United States many billions of dollars for our defense of them. Without us, gone!" Not every policy was new; like almost every candidate before him, he vowed to move America's embassy in Israel from Tel Aviv to Jerusalem.

As president, Trump has done things differently than his predecessors. On 20 May 2017 Trump arrived in Saudi Arabia for his first trip abroad since taking office. He was the first president since Jimmy Carter not to visit Mexico or Canada on his first foreign trip. After this visit to Riyadh, Trump struck a different tone vis-a-vis Saudi Arabia. Trump's newfound appreciation for all policies Saudi may be attributable to the close relationship between Trump's son-in-law and senior advisor, Jared Kushner, and Saudi Crown Prince Mohammed bin Salman (MBS).

MBS is a reformer. Sort of. He has allowed women to drive in the kingdom, but arrested the women's rights activists who lobbied for that right. He allowed the first cinema to open in more than 30 years on 17 April 2018 with a showing of Black Panther, but has his critics arrested. He has also pursued an aggressive foreign policy that drew in the US on multiple fronts.

In Yemen, MBS has overseen a proxy war with Iranian-backed Houthi rebels. This war has killed more than 10,000 and brought millions to the brink of starvation (Al-Mujahed and Raghavan 2018, par. 8). The US has backed the Saudis in the Yemen conflict. The Center for Strategic and International Studies reports that, "The majority of US assistance has consisted of aerial targeting assistance, intelligence sharing, and mid-flight aerial refueling for Saudi and UAE aircraft" (Dalton et al. 2018, par. 4). While there is little chance that American ground forces will enter Yemen, support for Saudi Arabia in Yemen has become increasingly controversial.

US support for Saudi Arabia is not a Trump innovation. On 14 March 2011 Saudi troops crossed the causeway into Bahrain to help suppress an uprising by the majority Shia population against the minority Sunni al-Khalifa rulers. The Obama Administration did not get directly involved, but expressed its support for the al-Khalifas. The Trump Administration went a step further by lifting human rights restrictions on arms sales to Bahrain.

Trump took support for Saudi Arabia to new heights in his support for Riyadh in the 2017 Gulf Cooperation Council (GCC) crisis. The crisis began when hackers posted false, pro-Iran, statements by the Qatari Emir on the Qatar News Agency website. In response to these false statements, on 5 June 2017 Saudi Arabia announced a blockade of Qatar, which was soon joined by Bahrain, UAE, and Egypt. The next day Trump tweeted his support for the Saudis and implied that he accepted the Saudi position that Qatar supported terrorism, "So good to see the Saudi Arabia visit with the King and 50 countries already paying off. They said they would take a hard line on funding.... Perhaps this will be the beginning of the end to the horror of terrorism!" This statement took both the Qataris and the American defense establishment by surprise. Qatar's Al Udeid base is America's largest in the Middle East and Qatar and the US have extensive security cooperation. Al Udeid is critical to operations in Afghanistan, Iraq, Syria, and the entire region. The Trump Administration's position has since moderated and it has expressed support for Qatar and an end to the crisis. Nevertheless, the crisis continued into its second year.

Trump Reverses Obama-era policies

Trump has reversed a variety of Obama-era policies in the region. Obama's final decision on admitting refugees from the Syrian Civil War was to admit 110,000 of the 5.6 million who, according to the UN High Commissioner for Refugees, have fled Syria since 2011. President Trump reduced the number to 0. Trump not only barred Syrian refugees from entering the United States, he barred all citizens of Iraq, Iran, Libya, Somalia, Sudan, Syria and Yemen from entering the US.

In another policy reversal, Trump announced that the US would withdraw from the JCPOA. The US intelligence community and the IAEA assessed that Iran had been in full compliance with the JCPOA. Nevertheless, Trump, having repeatedly called the JCPOA "the worst deal ever negotiated," decided to withdraw from the agreement (Delk 2018, par. 3). The full impact of that decision is not yet known. And in Israel, Trump formally moved the US embassy from Tel Aviv to Jerusalem.

Conclusion

The US began the post-Cold War era in the Middle East in an enviable position. It had widespread public and elite support. The region had never been quiet, but the coalition against Saddam Hussein had united disparate actors and there was reason to hope for future cooperation. The United States had never been entirely absent from the Middle East, but 30 years of interventions and more than 17 years of war left both America and the Middle East with countless unresolved, and perhaps unresolvable, problems.

The author would like to thank Mashell Rahimzadeh and Nada Osman for their valuable assistance on this chapter.

References

107th Congress. 2001. "PUBLIC LAW 107–40—SEPT. 18, 2001: Joint Resolution." *Government Publishing Office,* September 18, 2001. https://www.gpo.gov/fdsys/pkg/PLAW-107publ40/pdf/PLAW-107publ40.pdf

Blair, David. 2016. "The Gulf War Marked the Pinnacle of American Military Supremacy." *Telegraph,* January 17, 2016. https://www.telegraph.co.uk/news/worldnews/middleeast/iraq/12101906/The-Gulf-War-was-the-beginning-of-the-end-for-American-supremacy.html

Breslow, Jason M. 2016. "Colin Powell: U.N Speech Was a Great Intelligence Failure." *PBS: Frontline,* May 17, 2016. https://www.pbs.org/wgbh/frontline/article/colin-powell-u-n-speech-was-a-great-intelligence-failure/

Bush, George W. 2001. "Text: President Bush Addresses the Nation." *Washington Post,* September 20, 2001. http://www.washingtonpost.com/wp-srv/nation/specials/attacked/transcripts/bushaddress_092001.html?noredirect=on

"Bush on Iraq: What Did Dad Say?" *United Press International,* September 23, 2003. https://www.upi.com/Bush-on-Iraq-What-did-Dad-say/33521064337580/

Cheney, Dick and Tim Russert. 2003. "Transcript for Sept. 14." *National Broadcasting Company (NBC),* September 14, 2003. http://www.nbcnews.com/id/3080244/ns/meet_the_press/t/transcript-sept/#.Ww7ti0gvww

Conahan, Frank C. 1991. "Allied Contributions in Support of Operations Desert Shield and Desert Storm." *United States General Accounting Office.* July 31, 1991.

Dalton, Melissa, Hijab Shah, and Timothy Robbins. 2018. "U.S Support for Saudi Military Operations in Yemen." *Center for Strategic and International Affairs,* March 28, 2018. https://www.csis.org/analysis/us-support-saudi-military-operations-yemen

Delk, Josh. 2018. "Trump Aides Prepare for Iran Nuclear Deal Pullout: Report." *The Hill,* April 5, 2018. http://thehill.com/homenews/administration/381747-trump-aides-prepare-for-iran-nuclear-deal-pullout-report

Frank, Jeffrey. 2015. "Twenty-Five Years After Another Gulf War." *New Yorker,* July 16, 2015. https://www.newyorker.com/news/daily-comment/twenty-five-years-after-another-gulf-war

Haberman, Clyde. 1995. "Israeli Study Sees Higher Death Rate From '91 Scud Attacks." *New York Times,* April 21, 1995. https://www.nytimes.com/1995/04/21/world/israeli-study-sees-higher-death-rate-from-91-scud-attacks.html

Lizza, Ryan. 2011. "The Consequentialist." *New Yorker,* May 2, 2011. https://www.newyorker.com/magazine/2011/05/02/the-consequentialist

Mujahed, Ali, and Sudarsan Raghavan. 2018. "Yemen's War is Out of Control, Allies Turning on One Another." *Washington Post,* February 3, 2018. https://www.washingtonpost.com/world/yemens-war-is-so-out-of-control-that-allies-are-turning-on-one-another/2018/02/03/50d26426-05fe-11e8-aa61-f3391373867e_story.html?utm_term=.df4f5fedecb9

Obama, Barack. 2013. "Transcript: President Obama's Aug. 31 Statement on Syria." *Washington Post,* August 31, 2013. https://www.washingtonpost.com/politics/transcript-president-obamas-aug-31-statement-on-syria/2013/08/31/3019213c-125d-11e3-b4cb-fd7ce041d814_story.html?utm_term=.14b4b416cc60

Powell, Colin. 2003. "Transcript of Powell's U.N Presentation: Part 2: Hiding Prohibited Equipment." *Central News Network,* February 5, 2003. http://edition.cnn.com/2003/US/02/05/sprj.irq.powell.transcript/index.html

Pressman, Jeremy. 2003. "Visions in Collision: What Happened at Camp David and Taba" *International Security,* 28. no. 2. (Fall 2003): 5–43.

Reuters Staff. 2018. "Trump Thanks Qatar for Efforts to Combat Terrorism." *Reuters,* January 15, 2018. https://www.reuters.com/article/us-gulf-qatar-usa/trump-thanks-qatar-for-efforts-to-combat-terrorism-idUSKBN1F42HT

Sanchez, Raf. 2016. "Iran-backed Shia militia says it will fight US Marines deployed to Iraq." *Telegraph,* March 21, 2016. https://www.telegraph.co.uk/news/worldnews/middleeast/iraq/12200172/Iran-backed-Shia-militia-says-it-will-fight-US-Marines-deployed-to-Iraq.html

Sly, Liz. 2015. "The Hidden Hand Behind Islamic State Militants? Saddam Hussein's." *Washington Post,* April 4, 2015. https://www.washingtonpost.com/world/middle_east/the-hidden-hand-behind-the-islamic-state-militants-saddam-husseins/2015/04/04/aa97676c-cc32-11e4-8730-4f473416e759_story.html?utm_term=.38a6e5188be2

The Associated Press. 2016. "Timeline of U.S Troops level in Afghanistan since 2001." *Military Times,* July 6, 2016. https://www.militarytimes.com/news/your-military/2016/07/06/a-timeline-of-u-s-troop-levels-in-afghanistan-since-2001/

Trump, Donald (@realdonaldtrump). 2015. "Saudi Arabia should be paying the United States many billions of dollars for our defense of them. Without us, gone! @AlWaleedbinT" Twitter, June 29, 2015, 4:40 am. https://twitter.com/realdonaldtrump/status/615485019503620097

Trump, Donald (@realdonaldtrump). 2017. "So good to see the Saudi Arabia visit with the King and 50 countries already paying off. They said they would take a hard line on funding…" Twitter, June 6, 2017, 6:36 am. https://twitter.com/realdonaldtrump/status/872084870620520448?lang=en

UNHCR. 2018. "Syria Emergency." Emergencies. Last modified April 19, 2018. http://www.unhcr.org/en-us/syria-emergency.html

United Nations Security Council. 1990. "Resolution 660." *Security Council Resolutions-1990,* August 2, 1990. http://www.un.org/Docs/scres/1990/scres90.htm

United Nations Security Council. 1990. "Resolution 678: Iraq-Kuwait." *Security Council Resolutions,* November 29, 1990. http://unscr.com/en/resolutions/678

Weed, Matthew. 2016. "Presidential References to the 2001 Authorization for Use of Military Force in Publicly Available Executive Actions and Reports to Congress." *Congressional Research Service,* May 11, 2016. https://fas.org/sgp/crs/natsec/pres-aumf.pdf

Weiner, Tim. 1993. "Patriot Missile Success A Myth, Israeli Aides Say." *New York Times.* November 21, 1993. https://www.nytimes.com/1993/11/21/world/patriot-missile-s-success-a-myth-israeli-aides-say.html

World Islamic Front. 1998. "Jihad Against Jews and Crusaders." *9/11 Memorial,* February 23, 1998. https://www.911memorial.org/sites/default/files/Osama%20bin%20Laden's%201998%20Fatwa%20declaring%20war%20against%20the%20West%20and%20Israel.pdf

4

Russian Foreign Policy in the Middle East under Putin: Can Bears Walk in the Desert?

SPYRIDON N. LITSAS

In 1787, the Russian Empress Catherine II visited Crimea with several European ambassadors. The purpose of the trip was to impress and deceive the ambassadors regarding the true power capacity of Russia prior to a new war against the Sublime Porte. For that purpose, Grigory Potemkin, governor of Crimea, set up mobile villages full of soldiers that were dressed as peasants in order to present a fake picture of a fully developed countryside with thriving agricultural activity. Since then 'Potemkin villages' became synonymous with diplomatic deception and influenced deeply the Russian foreign policy culture. As Vladimir Lukin notes, Russian Foreign policy has a "passion for mere show, the Potemkin village syndrome" (Lo 2002, 67).

Even during its imperial era, Russia showed an interest in the Middle East that had much to do with Moscow's soft-power expansionism in the region. This can be seen, for example, in the Kucuk Kaynarca Treaty in 1774 that not only tried to regulate the military tensions between the Ottoman and the Russian Empires but also granted the privilege to the latter to be acknowledged as the 'champion' of the Christian sites of worship in the Holy Land and beyond (Ismael, Ismael and Perry 2016, 33). Moscow, from the early days of the 18th century, fully acknowledged the geostrategic importance of the region and it also recognized its soft power leverage as a place where the three great monotheistic religions of the globe were in osmosis. Thus, it tried to take advantage of its Christian Orthodox doctrinal norm. However, imperial Russia developed a distinct hesitancy towards the prospect of antagonizing the European powers that had already placed the region under their own shadow. The main reason for this political indecisiveness was coming from the fact that for Russia the Balkans, the Caucasus region or Central Eastern Europe were much more important than the Middle East.

Characteristically, when in 1901 the Emir of Kuwait Mubarak al Sabah asked to be placed under Russian protection, the request was refused mainly because Russia did not want to antagonize Great Britain in the region (Kreutz 2007, 123). The same attitude, hesitance and self-restraint, was traceable during the Soviet era as well. The Middle East continued to appear in Soviet rhetoric as a region of primary geostrategic and geo-economic importance for Moscow. Additionally, the Kremlin tried to establish close ideological links with various Arab states by promoting and championing the Baathist ideology, accusing the Western world of neo-colonialism – while during the late stages of the British mandate in Palestine and the early period of the independent Israeli state it established close relations with the Haganah and later on with the Ben Gurion administration (Sicker 2000, 213–215). Again, these moves must be seen as indirect attempts to challenge the British and American presence in the region and not as efforts to revise, directly or indirectly, the regional status quo. This Soviet attitude can also be detected during the rise of the Baathist and Nasserist political movements in Iraq, Syria and Egypt (Dawisha 2016) which were blends of Arab nationalism with large doses of third world socialism.

The aforementioned regimes had developed close relations with the Soviet Union either as associates or as the Kremlin's puppets in the Middle East. Despite the fact that through this ideological and in some case economic and military patronage Moscow had an excellent opportunity to undermine the Western presence there, it did not want to elevate antagonism in the Middle East to a higher level. On the contrary, the Soviet approach was mainly focused on weakening the ties between the United States and the Arab states instead of establishing its own sphere of influence. For example, Soviet proposals for the political neutralization of the Mediterranean and the Persian Gulf through a wide-scale demilitarization during the late 1970s and early 80s aimed to affect mainly US–Arab relations by presenting Moscow as the sole element who respects the Arab sovereignty and Washington as a firm aggressor (Allison 2009, 147–160). Moscow abandoned its traditional duplicitous Middle Eastern policy towards the Western world only during the last phase of the Soviet Union, when Mikhail Gorbachev understood that the USSR was economically and politically exhausted. Thus, the Soviet decision to condemn the Iraqi invasion of Kuwait and authorize military action against the Baathist regime by the US and its allies can be seen within this aforementioned context of Soviet weakness (Allison 2012, 157–161; Fuller 1991).

The Yeltsin Period: Playing Safe

As was expected, the collapse of the Soviet Union opened a wider discussion within the Russian political elite regarding the new Grand Strategy the state had to adopt in order to sail through the stormy waters of the post-Cold War international archipelago. A small part of the Russian political elite wanted to come closer to the US in order to achieve rapid economic recovery and domestic political stability. Another larger group wanted to adopt a balanced foreign policy, i.e. frequently siding with the US but also maintaining an independent approach where the Russian national interests were not in accordance with American ones. Last but not least, the most influential group was the nationalist side who wanted the adoption of a hardline policy against the US in general. The hardliners, a bizarre mixture of ultra-nationalists and ex-communist officials, demanded the return of Russia to the front row of international affairs (Freedman 2001). According to them, this could be attained only through a new round of direct antagonism with the US.

Boris Yeltsin, the first president of the Russian Federation (1991–1999), opted to not openly challenge the US. Nevertheless, he continued with the traditional Russian policy in the Middle East of not following an aggressive line towards regional developments. He was also concerned not to miss any opportunity to indirectly challenge the established American policy. Therefore, Yeltsin's Russia participated in the signing ceremonies of the 1993 Oslo Accords between Israel and the Palestinian administration and in the signing of the 1994 Peace Treaty between Israel and Jordan – two pivotal diplomatic initiatives of the US State Department aimed at the establishment of a more stable balance of power in the Middle East. Yet, it was Yeltsin's Russia that called for the lifting of the international sanctions against Iraq and Libya in 1994, a diplomatic move that irritated the US and made Moscow popular again within the anti-Western Arab nucleus (Felkay 2002, 82). During the same period, Moscow tried to play a stabilizing role between Israel and the Palestinians. In November 1996 and in October 1997 Evgenii Primakov, the Russian Minister of Foreign Affairs, visited both Israel and the Palestinian authority in an attempt to portray to the rest of the world that Moscow was ready to take every necessary step in order to contribute to a viable peace settlement. During his second visit in Israel, Primakov transmitted messages between the Israeli Premier Benjamin Netanyahu and the Syrian President Hafez Al-Assad to show the Israeli side that Moscow was able to influence Syrian foreign policy in favor of a new status between the two sides (Feldman 1998). In addition, during the Lebanese crisis of 1997, Moscow approached Syria and Iran and asked both states to terminate their support for Hezbollah. Nevertheless, it was not long before Russia sealed a $2 billion arms deal with Syria giving it the opportunity to carry on with its destabilizing policies towards Lebanon (Feldman 1998).

Yeltsin's era and its policy line towards the Middle East can be seen as a first step towards a Russian foreign policy of getting back to normality. In addition, it can be labeled as a mild-smart policy that tried on the one hand to minimize the cost for preserving a Russian political presence in the Middle East and extending on the other hand the attrition for Washington at every given opportunity. The Russian navy was not yet in the position to antagonize the Sixth Fleet of the US, while the Kremlin was also struggling hard to face the dire consequences of the Soviet economic and social failures and at the same time maintain influence over pivotal regions such as the Caucasus. Nevertheless, Yeltsin saw the Middle Eastern conundrum as the ideal venue in order to exercise a non-costly yet ambitious foreign policy. Thus, Russia tried to be present in each and every important development that occurred in the region during the first phase of the post-Cold War period to show to the rest of the world that despite the Soviet collapse, Russia was still a major international actor. Yet, in reality Russia did not have the capacity to follow such an ambitious foreign policy. So, Russia resorted once again to the Potemkin deception. By showing public disapproval at the UN Security Council towards certain US Foreign Policy moves in the Middle East – such as economic sanctions against Iraq or the close relations between Washington and the Gulf states on regulating oil prices – Russia was trying to distinguish itself within the international community. It was a good plan that yielded some successful results. However, it was widely known that Russia could not survive without US economic aid and thus few paid any close attention to the Russian Middle East Potemkin villages.

The Putin Era: A New Offensive Stance

The arrival of Vladimir Putin, first as a Prime Minister and then as President came with a conservative stance, preserving the fundamental lines of Yeltsin's Russian Foreign Policy. In the Middle East, the main preoccupation of the new administration was to prevent the transmission of regional crises to the nucleus of the Russian Federation, e.g. the rise of jihadism. Since his early days in office Putin faced jihadism in Chechnya and in other neighboring territories. Simultaneously, the strengthening of the Taliban regime and al-Qaeda's influence in Afghanistan applied considerable pressure upon the Kremlin. As Oded Eran describes Putin's early days:

> Relating specifically to the Middle East, what transpires is that Russia's top objective in that geographical space is political stabilization for the purpose of forestalling the spillover of political and military crises, endemic to the region into the volatile regions of central Asia and the Caucasus, inside Russia and out, in its 'near abroad' (Eran 2003, 159).

Putin, well experienced in security issues, was fully aware of the open links of communication between Arab jihadists and Salafist groups in the Caucasus region. For this reason, he approached the Middle East as the main corridor for terrorists wanting to penetrate the Russian domain. Additionally, political stability in the Caucasus was, and still is, vital for Moscow for the uninterrupted transport of Caspian oil and gas to the European and Asian markets. Nevertheless, regarding the so-called *'Big Game'* – US–Russian antagonism – he decided to continue Yeltsin's policy in an attempt to challenge US presence in the Middle East whenever that was feasible. These challenges adopted the form of either the reinforcement of diplomatic and military links between Moscow and various rogue Arab states with a profound anti-Western agenda such as Iraq, Libya and Syria, or they were expressed through Moscow's unwillingness to work with Western powers in order to achieve wider regional stability. For example, during the 2006 Hezbollah–Israel clashes Moscow drew a separate line from the Western world. Instead of offering its uncompromised support to Jerusalem, it maintained open channels of communications with Hezbollah's leader, Hassan Nasrallah (Katz and Pollak 2015).

In general, during these early days in office Putin tried not to alarm the US too much in an attempt to win some time and heal as many wounds as he could of the almost incapacitated post-Yeltsin Russian bureaucratic apparatus. 9/11 and what followed gave Putin an unexpected opportunity to modify his primary foreign policy stance and move ahead in various regions of strategic importance, including the Middle East. The decision of the White House not only to conduct a full-scale war against al-Qaeda and the Taliban in Afghanistan but to neutralize jihadism globally reveals the American spirits after 9/11. The Bush administration (2001–2009) decided that it was vital for the security of the US not only to end the tyrannical regimes of Saddam Hussein in Iraq and that of the Taliban in Afghanistan, but to generate a broader change of paradigm in the Middle East through the implementation of the so-called Democratic Peace Theory. The Bush administration chose to introduce this post-Kantian approach as the corner stone of its counterinsurgency strategy in the Middle East – an effort that cost trillions and almost impaired the American economy. The gigantic economic effort to withstand the maximalism of Bush's administration forced Barack Obama's administration (2009–2017) to change the US strategic commitments. The American electorate had grown weary with military involvement in the Middle East, thus Obama issued a new strategic goal for the nation; the pivot to the Asia-Pacific. The United States continued to be interested in the socio-political developments in the Middle East, mainly due to the vital importance of the sea routes of the Mediterranean. However, this time there was no US willingness to be directly involved in the numerous regional conundrums. Nevertheless, politics, as nature, abhors a vacuum and Putin's Russia took full advantage of the US reorientation.

In the early days following 9/11 Putin proved to be a skillful artisan, balancing between the need to persuade the international system that Russia was willing to align with the Western world against the jihadists and with the decision to pursue his long-established strategy to challenge the American presence in the Middle East. Immediately after the 9/11 attacks Russia publicly offered its support to the US for the military operations in Afghanistan, while it also gave the US access to military bases in Tajikistan and Uzbekistan in order to conduct their aerial attacks against the Taliban (US Department of State Archive 2001–2003). However, in the summer and fall of 2002 Russia openly confronted the US over its Iraq policies. Russia not only opposed any discussion regarding the prospect of regime change in Iraq in various international venues, including inside the United Nations, but also provided political support to Saddam Hussein before and during the Iraq war of 2003 (Kramer 2006; Kanet 2010, 212). In the following years the distance between Washington and Moscow in the Middle East became more evident with Russia being less hesitant to reveal its true intentions against the US presence in the region. Nevertheless, it was not until the arrival of Obama's administration when Russia abandoned its conservative stance and adopted a more offensive approach that aimed not only to undermine US presence in the region but to expand its own.

Clearly, Russia was not willing to bandwagon with the US any more. The Russians, masters in the Potemkin diplomacy, knew very well that what matters most is what others think of your power capacity and not if you are truly willing to match your rhetoric with actions. Before the first US–Russian summit under the Obama administration in April 2009, Dmitry Medvedev, President of Russia during that time and one of the closest associates of Vladimir Putin, emphasized the need for equality and mutual benefits of the two great powers – since both Russia and the US had a special responsibility in world affairs concerning strategic stability and nuclear security (Oldberg 2010, 36–37). Moscow was sending the signal to the international system that it had not only returned back to the front row of the international arena but that it was also ready to match the United States in international affairs. The Middle East, together with Central Asia, were the ideal terrains for this.

The onset of the Arab Spring gave Russia the opportunity to put this new approach into action. In general terms, this new approach can be characterized as emphatically offensive and pragmatic in terms of comprehending the change in the regional balance of power – and moving accordingly. What Russia set out to do was to discover new territories in order to create a new sphere of influence. By doing that, the Kremlin aspired to expand its aura in the Eastern Mediterranean, on the one hand, while on the other hand it aimed to seize more opportunities in order to intervene – by proxy or directly – in various regional crises. As Ekaterina Stepanova notes:

> The main characteristics of Russia's policy in the Middle East, both before and after the outbreak of the Syrian crisis, have remained pragmatism, a non-ideological approach, and readiness to engage in selective cooperation with most regional actors, despite tensions between and even with them (Stepanova 2016).

At first, Russia approached the Arab Spring with a characteristic conspiratorial flair, seeing the various revolts in the Arab world as a violent process fabricated by the US in order to give the Kremlin the elbow from the region (Malashenko 2013, 9). Nevertheless, Moscow soon understood that the Arab Spring was an opportunity to implement its own pivot to the Middle East. Putin made an official opening to the Muslim Brotherhood by inviting Egypt's new President, Mohamed Morsi, to Moscow – despite of the fact that according to a 2003 Russian Supreme Court ruling, Morsi's Muslim Brotherhood was on the official list of terrorist organizations (Malashenko 2013, 9). This non-ideological pragmatism was also seen in the Libyan case, where Moscow showed that it was prepared to assist its old allies – yet it was also prepared to accept the new realities that were emerging from the outcome of the Arab Spring revisionist process too.

During the early stages of the Libyan crisis, the Russian side tried hard through diplomacy to achieve the continuation of the Qaddafi regime. Qaddafi had been a valuable ally in the region since the Cold War era, while Benghazi and Tobruk – two strategically situated port cities in the Eastern Mediterranean – were useful to the expansion of Russian naval hard power and the transformation of the Black Sea Fleet into a blue water force. However, when it became clear that Qaddafi had no future in Libya, the Russian delegation abstained in a UN Security Council vote that imposed a no-fly zone over Libya, prohibiting Qaddafi from using his air force to strike the rebels. This move, abstaining instead of rejecting, shows that after 9/11 Russia is seeing the Arab world with pragmatic eyes, searching for long-term political investments with the post-Arab Spring status quo that will eventually emerge in the region (Donaldson & Nogee 2014, 324). This is not necessarily a matter of breaking free from old bonds but reassessing the new realities in the Middle East and moving accordingly – including making swift changes when applicable.

However, the most characteristic case regarding the new Russian foreign policy in the Middle East can be found in Syria. Relations between Moscow and Damascus date back to the early post-1945 period and had been sealed with the granting of a small settlement in Tartus in 1971 that functioned as a Soviet naval military base with limited capacity. The beginning of the Syrian civil war offered Russia the opportunity to strengthen its ties with the Syrian regime and upgrade its military presence there. Besides the naval base in Tartus – that can today accommodate first and second rank ships from the Russia Mediterranean flotilla (Shlykov 2016, 35–38; Bodner 2015) – Russia *de facto* controls the strategic port of Latakia and the airbase at Hmeymin that has installed the notorious S-400 missile Triumf system. Meanwhile, Russian elite forces – the Spetsnaz – have taken part in various major operations against ISIS (Pleitgen 2016). The Syrian civil war presented an opportunity for Russia to lead a pro-Assad coalition, which involved building closer ties with Iran and Hezbollah. In sum, the Syrian civil war became a useful tool in the hands of Moscow in both short- and long-term ways.

Putin's Russia constantly tries to challenge the post-Cold War structural dimension of the international arena, that of systemic unipolarity and US power. According to Sergey Lavrov, the experienced Russian minister of foreign affairs and one of the closest Putin's associates, *"the international situation remains mosaic and controversial. Along with this, a common tendency could be observed…a polycentric international architecture"* (RT 2016). However, in order for Russia to support the existence of this new and dynamic polycentric international architecture it has to make known its own poles of influence. The Arab Spring's effect on the balance of power in the Middle East, and in particular the Syrian civil war that followed it, offered Russia the opportunity to not only effectuate Putin's goal of constructing a distinct pole of influence – but also to publicize to the world that Russia had re-emerged as a powerful global actor.

During the Arab Spring many analysts criticized the stance of the Obama administration regarding its non-support of traditional Western allies. The most characteristic case was that of Hosni Mubarak's regime in Egypt. Despite the fact that Mubarak was a significant US strategic partner, Obama decided not to intervene as Egypt underwent a revolution. In the face of the advice of his most experienced associates in foreign affairs – such as Hillary Clinton, Robert Gates and Tom Donilon who were strongly in favor of aiding Mubarak – Obama instead sided with his younger advisors who saw revolt as an opportunity for Egypt to follow a democratic path (Traub 2015). On top of that, the collapse of Mubarak's regime had been used by various analysts to devalue Obama's foreign policy credibility and discredit the national prestige of the US. For example, Raghida Dergam (2011) wrote in *Al Arabiya* that "the *Obama administration had become a liability to its friends,*" the editor of the *American Interest* Adam Garfinkle (2016) characterized the attitude of

Obama's administration towards the swift socio-political changes in the Middle East as 'Follyanna', while Zbiniew Brzezinski stated that "he doesn't strategize. He sermonizes" (Lizza 2011).

Putin found a window of opportunity in the Syrian crisis to boost Russian prestige by promoting the theory that Moscow never abandons its close allies and that states who get close to Russia can be protected by the Kremlin from domestic and international hazards. As the late Vitaly Churkin, the Russian representative in the United Nations for 11 years, stated during an interview with Colum Lynch (2015):

> We are stronger on our allegiances than others, I think, and this is being recognized internationally... if you have good relations with a country, a government, for years, for decades, then it's not so easy to ditch those politicians and those governments because of political expediency... Russia could be trusted more than the United States to back its friends.

It goes without saying that this strategy has already shown positive results. The current Egyptian President Abdel Fattah el-Sisi maintains close relations with Moscow, Saudi Arabia has upgraded its diplomacy with Russia, while Israel worked to build stronger links with Moscow during a period of US–Israel disharmony between the Netanyahu and Obama administrations. It has to be noted here that Donald Trump's administration has responded to the perceived failures of Obama and set out to make up lost ground. Trump quickly set about establishing a different pattern of relations with the pivotal states in the Middle East – including Israel and Egypt. In addition, the US bombing of the Syrian air base in Shayrat in April 2017 in response to a chemical weapons attack must also be seen as a US venture to discredit the Russian narrative and as a test to gauge the level of the Russian commitment to its support of Assad's regime.

Beyond the Middle East

One of the most urgent foreign policy goals for Russia is to face the strategic challenge of the activation of a land-based NATO missile system in Deveselu, Romania. The Deveselu military base hosts an Aegis system – a missile shield to protect NATO's European states from short and medium range missiles. The base, together with an analogous base in Poland, is set to play a decisive role in the European defense structure for decades to come. Russia considers both these military bases as a major security threat and thus tries to find suitable strategic alternatives in order to balance these hard power establishments. One of these strategic developments is the strengthening of the Russian Black Sea Fleet, which has been qualitatively and quantitatively upgraded. Russia can now potentially isolate Romania from its NATO allies by closing the entrance of the Black Sea to Western naval powers and at the same time open a parallel front in the Eastern Mediterranean. According to Stephen Black:

> These trends have allowed Russia to essentially make it extremely difficult, if not impossible, for NATO to get into the Black Sea to defend NATO allies and partners without substantial losses of ships, planes, and men (Coalson 2016).

Russia is aware that in order to broaden this strategic advantage, it has to preserve its presence in the Middle East – gradually transforming the region from a Western zone of influence to a ground of ideological and political antagonism between Washington and Moscow.

In addition, the strategic importance of the Middle East for Moscow adopted a parallel dimension that was seen during the Ukrainian crisis of 2013. Putin followed the traditional foreign line regarding the necessity of preserving Russian interests in its near abroad, which includes the Caucasus and Central and Eastern Europe. The main reason for this approach has to do with the fact that Russia has always felt vulnerable towards invasion due to the vast flat steppes that offer a strategic advantage to a foe who can enter the Russian heartland without having to face challenging terrain or high-rise mountains. Indeed, this has occurred twice; once during Napoleon's invasion in 1812 and again during the Nazi invasion in 1941. Naturally, this is just one dimension that draws on the psychology of the Russian consciousness as derived from the historical evolution of the Russian people and their land. The other dimension refers to the strategic fact that should Russia lose control (or influence) over the Caucasus and Central and Eastern Europe then access to the Mediterranean will be unattainable and eventually Russia will be isolated in Asia.

Russian fears have maximized after successive waves of EU and NATO enlargement, including the absorption of members of the ex-Warsaw Pact. This development has forced Russia to reconsider its attitude towards the Western world, while also offering an ideal opportunity to justify its propensity to violence every time it feels that vital Russian interests are in jeopardy. This posture manifested in 2008 during the Russian–Georgian war and then again when Russia invaded Ukraine in 2014 – ultimately leading to the annexation of Crimea. Putin is using the increasing Russian involvement in the Middle East to focus the Western gaze away from the Caucasus region and Central and Eastern Europe. Meanwhile he continues to make moves in the Middle

East such as with the signing of a $2.5 billion deal with Turkey for the purchase of the Russian S-400 'Triumf' missile defense system (Daniels 2017) and two major nuclear energy deals with Turkey and Egypt. On top of that, Putin made good strategic use of the Syrian civil war in order to drive the US and NATO to commit forces and resources into the region. Consequently, as the Syrian civil war has deepened, the US and NATO have placed Ukraine and Georgia on a high dusty shelf as their attention is monopolized by defeating the jihadists on the one hand and on the other hand controlling Russian involvement in the Arab world. It is more than clear that Putin sees the Middle East as an ideal boost for the Kremlin's status and a decoy that keeps antagonists away from Russia's spheres of influence in its near abroad.

Conclusion

The Middle East was never at the top of the Russian (or the Soviet) agenda until the arrival of Putin. However, following the 9/11 attacks – and in particular after the Arab Spring – Putin's Russia saw the Middle East's volatile condition as an excellent opportunity to expand its influence. At the same time, it was an ideal opportunity to keep the gaze of the Western world away from regions with greater strategic importance for the Kremlin such as the Caucasus and Central-Eastern Europe. Various analysts today claim that the international system has already entered into a new 'cold war' between the US and Russia. I disagree with these views, mainly because neither Washington nor Moscow have the appetite or the capacity to enter in such a holistic and demanding state of affairs. Nevertheless, Russia now follows a more aggressive policy in the Middle East and this is likely to continue as the region falls deeper into crisis. There are no more Potemikin villages in the Middle East. Instead, there are raw ambitions together with a profound Russian propensity for escalating antagonism with the West.

References

Allison, Roy. 2009. *The Soviet Union and the Strategy of non-alignment in the Third World*. Cambridge: Cambridge University Press.

Allison, William Thomas. 2012. *The Gulf War 1990–1991*. Basingstoke & New York: Palgrave Macmillan.

Belasco, Amy. 2008. 'The Cost of Iraq, Afghanistan, and Other Global War on Terror Operations Since 9/11', *Congressional Research Service Report*. https://fas.org/sgp/crs/natsec/RL33110.pdf

Bodner, Matthew. 2015. 'Why Russia is expanding its naval base in Syria', *The Moscow Times*, September 21, 2015. http://www.themoscowtimes.com/business/article/why-russia-is-expanding-its-syrian-naval-base/531986.html.

Coalson, Robert. 2016. 'Russian buildup focuses concerns around the Black Sea', *Radio Free Europe / Radio Liberty*, February 23, 2016. http://www.rferl.org/content/russia-black-sea-militarybuildup-turkey/27569877.html

Daniels, Jeff. 2017. 'US relays concern to Turkey after NATO ally makes deposit to buy Russian defense system', *CNBC*, September 12, 2017. https://www.cnbc.com/2017/09/12/us-turkish-ties-continue-to-deteriorate-.html

Dawisha, Adeed. 2016. *Arab Nationalism in the 20th century: From Triumph to Despair*. New Jersey, NY: Princeton University Press, new ed.

Dergham, Raghida. 2011. "The Obama Administration has become a liability to its friends". *Al Arabiya News*, February 12, 2011. https://www.alarabiya.net/views/2011/02/12/137295.html

Donaldson, H. Robert. & Jospeh L. Nogee. 2014. *The Foreign Policy of Russia: Changing Systems, Enduring Interests*. London: M.E.Sharpe, 2014, fifth ed.

Eran, Oded. 'Russia in the Middle East: The Yeltsin Era and Beyond'. In *Russia between East and West: Russian Foreign Policy on the Threshold of the 21st Century*, edited by Gabriel Gorodetsky, 159-170. London: Frank Cass, 2003.

Feldman, Shai. 1998. 'The Return of the Russian Bear', *Strategic Assessment*, 1, no. 1: 11–16.

Felkay, Andrew. 2002. *Yeltsin's Russia and the West*. Westport & London: Praeger.

Freedman, O. Robert. 2001. 'Russian Policy Towards the Middle East Under Yeltsin and Putin', *Jerusalem Center for Public Affairs*, 461. http://www.jcpa.org/jl/vp461.htm

Garfinkle, Adam. 2016. 'Follyanna?', *The American Interest*, February 11, 2016. https://www.the-american-interest.com/2016/02/11/follyanna/

Graham E. Fuller. 1991. 'Moscow and the Gulf War', *Foreign Affairs,* 70. https://www.foreignaffairs.com/articles/russia-fsu/1991-06-01/moscow-and-gulf-war

Kanet, E. Roger. 2010. 'From the 'New World Order' to 'Resettling Relations': Two decades of US-Russian Relations'. In *Russian Foreign Policy in the 21st Century*, edited by Roger E. Kanet, 204–227. New York: Palgrave Macmillan.

Katz, Muni and Pollak, Navak. 2015. 'Hezbollah's Russian Military Education in Syria', *The Washington Institute*. http://www.washingtoninstitute.org/policy-analysis/view/hezbollahs-russian-military-education-in-syria

Kramer, Mark. 2006. 'Did Russia help Saddam during the war?', *Washington Post,* April 2, 2006. http://www.washingtonpost.com/wpdyn/content/article/2006/03/31/AR2006033102288.html.

Kreutz, Andrej. 2007. *Russia in the Middle East: Friend or Foe?* Westport, CT: Praeger Security International.

Layne, Christopher. 1994. "Can't or Kant: The Myth of the Democratic Peace", *International Security*, 19, no.2: 5–49.

Litsas, N. Spyridon. 2012. 'Democratic Peace Theory and Militarism: The Unrelated Connectivity', *Civitas Gentium* 2, no.1: 33–58.

Lizza, Ryann. 2011. 'The Consequentialist: How the Arab Spring remade Obama's Foreign Policy', *The New Yorker*, May 2, 2011. http://www.newyorker.com/magazine/2011/05/02/the-consequentialist

Lo, Bobo. 2002. 'Illusion and Mythmaking'. In *Russian Foreign Policy in the post-Soviet Era: Reality, Illusion and Mythmaking*, edited by Bobo Lo, 66–97. New York: Palgrave Macmillan.

Lynch, Colum. 2015. 'Why Putin is so committed to Keeping Assad in Power', *Foreign Policy*, October 7, 2015. http://foreignpolicy.com/2015/10/07/putins-russia-is-wedded-to-bashar-al-assad-syria-moscow/

Malashenko, Alexey. 2013. *Russia and the Arab Spring*. Moscow: Carnegie Moscow Center.

Marshall, Tim. 2015. 'Russia and curse of Geography', *The Atlantic*, October 31, 2015. https://www.theatlantic.com/international/archive/2015/10/russia-geography-ukraine-syria/413248/.

Oldberg, Ingmar. 2010. Aims and Means in Russian Foreign Policy. In *Russian Foreign Policy in the 21st Century*, edited by Roger E. Kanet, 30–58. New York: Palgrave Macmillan.

Pleitgen, Frederik. 2016. 'Russia's military in Syria: Bigger than you think and not going anywhere', *CNN*, May 9, 2016. http://edition.cnn.com/2016/05/09/middleeast/russia-military-syria/.

RT. 2016. 'Shift to multipolar world: Lavrov says Russia working to adjust foreign policy to new reality', April 10, 2016. https://www.rt.com/news/339082-russia-new-foreign-policy-multipolar/.

Shlykov, Pavel. 2016. 'Russian foreign policy in the Eastern Mediterranean since 1991'. In *The Eastern Mediterranean in Transition: Multipolarity, Politics and Power*, edited by Spyridon N. Litsas & Aristotelis Tziampiris, 31–50. London & New York: Routledge, 2016.

Sicker, Martin. 2000. *Pangs of the Messiah: The Troubled Birth of the Jewish State*. Westport, CT: Greenwood Publishing Group.

Stepanova, Ekaterina. 2016. 'Russia in the Middle East: Back to a "Grand Strategy" or Enforcing Multirateralism?; *Politique Entragere*. http://www.cairn-int.info/article-E_PE_162_0023--russia-in-the-middle-east.htm#re2no2

Tareq, Ismael, Jacqueline S. Ismael & Glen E. Perry. 2016. *Government and Politics of the Contemporary Middle East: Continuity and Change*. London: Routledge.

Traub, James. 2015. 'The Hillary Clinton Doctrine', *Foreign Policy*, June 11, 2015. http://foreignpolicy.com/2015/11/06/hillary-clinton-doctrine-obama-interventionist-tough-minded-president/.

US Department of State Archive. 'The United States and the Global Coalition Against Terrorism September 2001–December 2003'. https://2001-2009.state.gov/r/pa/ho/pubs/fs/5889.htm.

5

China in the Post-Hegemonic Middle East: A Wary Dragon?

XI CHEN

The Middle East has been a historically contested ground for intertwined and conflicting interests. The gradual US withdrawal from the region combined with China's growing economic interests; Beijing's more confident stance towards foreign interactions; as well as China's "One Belt, One Road" (OBOR) initiative since 2013, have resulted in rising speculation about the trajectory of bilateral relations between China and the nations of the Middle East. Specifically, there is a rising voice arguing that China is developing a grand new Arab policy and actively pivoting towards the Middle East in order to fill the power vacuum left by US withdrawal (Ghosal 2016; Dusek and Kaiouz 2017; Luft 2016; Hayoun 2016; Romaniuk and Burgers 2016). On the other hand, there are scholars challenging the shifting nature of China's Middle East Policy, arguing that Beijing's policy towards the Middle East is driven by its domestic economic needs and China's military and diplomatic involvements in the region are superficial and symbolic at best (Scobell and Nader 2016; Calabrese 2017).

China's engagement with the Middle East has expanded dramatically since the end of the Cold War. With China's growing energy demands, Beijing's economic engagement with the region has further amplified during the past years. Most recently, 2016 marked a milestone in China–Middle East relations with a series of unusual political moves by Beijing, including Beijing's release of the first Arab Policy Paper on 13 January (State Council of the PRC 2016), Chinese President Xi Jinping's first trip to the Middle East countries of Saudi Arabia, Egypt, and Iran during January 19–23 (Xinhuanet 2016), as well as China's self-interpretation of the trip as a new type of international relations and diplomacy (Xinhuanet 2016; Xu 2016). These prominent signs of change seem to suggest a changed policy towards the region. They also raise a series of questions: Is China's Middle East Policy going through drastic changes? Towards which direction is it evolving? To what extent is Beijing pivoting towards the Middle East? Is Xi Jinping's China actively filling the power vacuum in the Middle East left by the US? Or has Beijing primarily continued its non-interference foreign policy? And finally, what does the Middle East mean to today's China politically, economically, and strategically? This research explores these questions via archival research and analysis of government documents and the official rhetoric of the Xi Jinping administration. By exploring the existing literature, government documents/data, official Xinhua news reports, as well as speeches/talks delivered by Chinese government officials since 2013 specifically, the research maps out the dynamics of China's engagement with the Middle East in a broader historical context.

The History of China–Middle East Relations

Despite over 2000 years of recorded history of bilateral engagement and interactions (Gao 2015; Scobell and Nader 2016), the exchange between the two entities has not always been smooth (Ma 2010). While the 1955 Bandung Asian–African Conference first kindled bilateral interactions between the People's Republic of China and Middle Eastern countries such as Egypt, Syria, and Yemen, the Sino–Soviet split (1956–1966) and the Chinese Cultural Revolution disrupted relations (Olimat 2014). The two parties did not resume interactions until the early 1970s when the PRC was admitted into the United Nations (UN), thus resulting in the establishment of diplomatic ties between China and Iran, Kuwait, Lebanon, Jordan, and Turkey (Shicor 1979). Under Deng Xiaoping, China's diplomatic success reached another height as Beijing established diplomatic relations with all Middle Eastern countries in the 1990s. China's rapidly growing economy offered products and opportunities. Middle Eastern countries, in turn, helped China fulfill its soaring need for energy and resources.

Although the Middle East became deeply embroiled in military conflicts fueled by the US at the beginning of the new millennium, relations between China and the region remained strong. With growing economic interests, China created the China–Arab States Cooperation Forum (CASCF) in 2004, which aims to "serve as a platform for exchanging views between China and Arab nations, promoting cooperation in politics, the economy and trade, culture, technology and international affairs while advancing peace and development" (Xinhuanet 2016). Since then, the forum has functioned as an important mechanism facilitating trade and cooperation between the two sides. Despite twists and turns in bilateral relations, Beijing has consistently upheld its official rhetoric of non-interference and non-intervention in regional internal affairs. This staunch neutrality, however, was put to the test in recent years due to significant changes in both China's domestic politics and the regional situation in the Middle East.

Recent Dynamics in China–Middle East Relations

With Xi's rise to power, China formally departed from Deng Xiaoping's world view of "keeping a low profile". The *One Belt One Road* (OBOR) initiative proposed by Xi in 2013 was believed to substantively "expand China's economic and diplomatic influence over the Middle East at the expense of the US supremacy" (Chaziza 2016; Xinhuanet 2016; Sharma and Kundu 2016). China's growing political and economic interests in the region increased the need and urgency for China to enhance its engagement with the Middle East. Additionally, rising domestic challenges such as domestic Islamic terrorism and economic rebalancing also push China towards greater engagement and closer cooperation with the region. As China acquired the status of a newly self-conscious power under Xi (Dittmer 2015), this newly assumed and more assertive national identity also raised expectations for Beijing to shoulder more responsibilities in regional and international affairs, thus putting pressures on China to participate in more substantive ways in constructing peace in the Middle East. As the research reveals, China's engagement with the Middle East under Xi has proliferated in both volume and significance and Beijing's interactions with the region have expanded economically, diplomatically, militarily and culturally.

Economic Engagement

According to the US Energy Information Administration, China overtook the US as the largest net importer of crude oil from the Middle East in 2013 and it again surpassed the US by becoming the largest importer or crude oil worldwide in 2017 (EIA 2018). Although China has attempted to diversify its sources of oil from non-OPEC countries over the past decade, by 2030, the Middle East is expected to account for 70 percent of China's energy needs (Olimat 2014). As significant as this statistic is, China's economic engagement with the Middle East goes far beyond the energy field. Driven by China's OBOR initiative and facilitated by the CASCF, China is engaging the region in multiple areas. In 2014, China proposed a "1+2+3" model of cooperation with the Middle East in the 6th Ministerial Conference of the China–Arab Forum. The proposal expanded bilateral cooperation from energy into diverse areas such as infrastructure, trade, and investment – as well as high tech cooperation in nuclear energy, space satellites, and other new energy initiatives. As the proposal materialized, China's investment in the region soared (Arun 2018). China's investment in Iraq's oil industry and its bilateral trade with Saudi Arabia are among the most noteworthy (Reuters 2015; State Council of the PRC 2015; Jin 2016; Erdbrink 2016; Ghosal 2016). In addition to an extensive cooperation on oil and energy, China and Saudi Arabia vowed to develop comprehensive strategic partnerships and cooperation in the fields of aerospace, finance, and nuclear power. In 2016 the two states established a bilateral mechanism, the China–Saudi Arabia High Level Joint Committee to facilitate the comprehensive partnership. In all, the whirlwind diplomacy conducted during Xi's first trip to the Middle East in 2016 secured no fewer than 50 cooperation agreements and memorandums of understanding (MOUs) with Middle East countries (Perlez 2016; Su 2016; Xinhuanet 2016).

China has also expanded economic cooperation with Palestine and Israel in recent years. Chinese officials including President Xi Jinping, Chinese Premier Li Keqiang, as well as foreign minister Wang Yi invariably reiterated China's commitment to deepening economic cooperation with both Israel and Palestine during official visits paid by Israel's Prime Minister Benjamin Netanyahu and Palestine's President Mahmoud Abbas in 2017 (Foreign Ministry of the PRC [FMPRC] 2017). Specifically, China announced its commitment to actively speed up negotiations on a China–Israel free trade zone. The two sides discussed deepening their collaboration in multiple areas ranging from advanced technology, clean energy, and communications. Israel also extended an invitation for China to participate in infrastructure construction projects in Israel (FMPRC 2017). With regard to Palestine, China committed to assist Palestine in increasing its self-help capacity by building industrial parks, developing solar power stations, and increasing investment and economic aid (FMPRC 2017). Both Israel and Palestine confirmed their eagerness to jointly build OBOR with China (FMPRC 2017).

The OBOR is expected to be the driving force of closer China–Middle East ties. At the time of writing, the Xi administration has stated that over 100 countries have welcomed the OBOR initiative and over 40 countries and international organizations have signed bilateral agreements with China to jointly build the OBOR. Moreover, China's investment in the countries along the OBOR route already reached $50 billion at the beginning of 2017 (N.D. 2017). As of now, major regional powers including Israel, Saudi Arabia, Turkey, and Iran all stand ready to jointly build the OBOR with China and many of these countries have taken practical steps to be part of this grand initiative. In September 2017, Iran's Foreign Minister Mohammad Javad Zarif commented during a visit to Beijing that Iran hoped to conduct integration with the Chinese side as soon as possible (FMPRC 2017). In late 2017, King Salman bin Abdulaziz Al Saud of Saudi Arabia also expressed Saudi Arabia's eagerness to integrate Saudi Arabia's Vision 2030 with the Belt and Road Initiative through the China–Saudi Arabia High Level Joint Committee in Beijing.

Diplomatic Engagement

Prominent Chinese diplomatic activities in the Middle East are commonplace during the Xi administration, with China playing an increasing role of peace mediator or peace broker for major conflicts in the region. China mediated the Yemen Crisis by hosting talks between Iran and Saudi Arabia during 2015–2016 (Middle East Observer, 2016). In December 2017, China hosted the "Palestinian–Israeli Peace Symposium" (Xinhuanet 2017). In May 2018, China also hosted the International Symposium on Syrian issues (FMPRC 2018). As part of the mediation efforts, China's special envoy to the Middle East made extensive visits to relevant countries to facilitate peace talks and political settlements during both the Libya and Syrian crisis (FMPRC, 2017). With regard to the Iran Nuclear Crisis, Beijing both facilitated and supported the Joint Comprehensive Plan of Action (JCPOA) via its bilateral consultation mechanism with Iran (FMPRC 2017).

Above and beyond being a peace mediator or broker, China also attempts to actively shape affairs by being more assertive in the UN Security Council – including by using multiple vetoes on the Syrian crisis – and by sharing Chinese wisdom in managing Middle East conflicts. After initially sharing a four point proposal in resolving the Syrian crisis in 2012, Chinese officials have repeatedly reiterated the "China approach" which emphasizes political, inclusive, and transitional means of managing the Syrian crisis. Beijing also made timely adjustments to its Syrian approach as the situation in the country changed. For example, in November 2017, Chinese Foreign Minister, Wang Yi, proposed counter-terrorism, dialogue and reconstruction as three key points for solving the Syrian crisis (FMPRC 2017).

In the case of the Israel–Palestine Conflict, Xi proposed a four point approach to Mahmoud Abbas in July 2017 promoting political settlement of the issue. The four points are advancing the Two-State Solution based on 1967 borders; upholding the concept of common, comprehensive, co-operative and sustainable security, immediately ending Israeli settlement building, taking immediate measures to prevent violence against civilians, and calling for an early resumption of peace talks; coordinating international efforts to put forward peace promoting measures that entail joint participation at an early date; as well as promoting peace through development and cooperation between the Palestinians and Israel. Additionally, Xi also proposed a China–Palestine–Israel trilateral dialogue mechanism shortly afterward (FMPRC 2017). Throughout the process of mediation between Palestine and Israel, China has consistently upheld the Two-State Solution and supported the establishment of a Palestinian state enjoying full sovereignty and independence on the basis of the 1967 borders with East Jerusalem as its capital

(FMPRC 2017). More widely, China has engaged in political consultations with a wide range of states and organizations like Turkey, Iran, France, Israel, the Arab League, the EU, the BRICS, as well as the UN in mediating peace in the Middle East.

China under Xi has clearly augmented its engagement with the region diplomatically at an unprecedented level. This diplomatic activism, however, should not be exaggerated as a hegemonic Chinese aspiration to replace the US in the Middle East. The very fact that China has consistently maintained its neutral position towards the Yemen Crisis, the Palestine–Israel Conflict, and the Syria and Libya Crises clearly shows China's efforts to avoid the interventionist US path in the region. On multiple occasions, Chinese officials emphasized that China had no private interests in the Middle East and the country stood ready to play a constructive role in the Middle East by upholding an unbiased and objective position on the regional affairs. In Xi's speech to the Arab League in 2016, he reiterated this:

> Instead of looking for a proxy in the Middle East, we promote peace talks; instead of seeking any sphere of influence, we call on all parties to join the circle of friends for the Belt and Road Initiative; instead of attempting to fill the "vacuum", we build a cooperative partnership network for win–win outcomes (Xinhua 2016).

In the same speech, Xi stressed that China would strive to be constructor of the Middle East peace, promoter of Middle East development, propeller of Middle East industrialization, supporter of Middle East stability, as well as a partner of Middle Eastern public diplomacy (N.D. 2017). The following year, Chinese Foreign Minister Wang Yi, further reiterated Beijing's stance at a joint press conference held with the Foreign Minister of Palestine:

> China has no geopolitical consideration in its role in the Middle East, nor intention to make a balance with any other country. We always propose historical justice and uphold international righteousness in the Middle East issue. China welcomes any country outside the region including the US that wants to support the Middle East more, and give more attention to the Palestine–Israel issue (FMPRC 2017).

Wang Yi further expounded China's position at the joint press conference with the Jordanian Minister of Foreign Affairs and Expatriates, Ayman Safadi, three months later:

China's role in the Middle East issue is definitely a constructive one. China pursues no geographical interests and seeks no sphere of influence in the Middle East, and will not be partial to any party. The Chinese side stands ready to adhere to the objective and impartial stance to push forward the political settlement of regional hotspot issues (FMPRC 2017).

Military Engagement

Besides flourishing economic and diplomatic activities, China has engaged the region militarily via arms sales, the presence of its navy forces, its participation in peacekeeping, and its collaboration with the regional anti-terrorism fight (Olimat 2014). Driven by the security challenges posed by extremists among the Chinese Muslims in Xinjiang, China passed its first anti-terrorism law in December 2015 paving the way for an active military involvement in anti-terror missions at home and abroad. Under the framework of bilateral cooperation, China actively supported Iraq in its fight against ISIS by sharing intelligence and providing training (Chaziza 2016). Additionally, military cooperation with Iran also expanded when the two countries held a joint military exercise in the Persian Gulf in June 2017 (South China Morning Post, 2017). China also held a joint anti-terrorism military exercise with Saudi Arabia in Chongqing, China. To contain the threat posed by the East Turkestan Islamic Movement (ETIM), China also actively sought enhanced counter-terrorism cooperation with Turkey (Reuters 2017). On top of this, Xi earmarked $300 million in aid to the Arab League in 2016 to enhance the capacity of the member states in preserving regional stability (N.D. 2017).

China's increased military collaborations across the Middle East went hand-in-hand with Xi's initiative to modernize China's military and increase Chinese military participation in global governance. Since Xi took office in 2013, he has emphasized the importance of modernizing the Chinese military in general and strengthening the navy in particular (N.D. 2017). China's military modernization is proceeding faster than expected to the extent that "it is China and no longer Russia, that increasingly provides the benchmark against which Washington judges the capability requirements for its own armed forces" (Marcus 2018). As part of comprehensive efforts to improve military management and capacity, China has formed a Ministry of Veterans Affairs in March 2018 and has committed itself to more extensive financial and personnel participation in UN peacekeeping endeavors. Despite the burgeoning military collaboration with Middle Eastern countries on the anti-terrorism front, it is noteworthy that China remains reluctant to align with any state militarily in the region. According to China's Foreign Minister, Wang Yi, "China will not take part in any coalition fighting 'terrorist groups' in the Middle

East, but will do its fair share in its own way." (Irish 2016).

Cultural Engagement

China has vigorously promoted cultural exchanges with the Middle East under the Xi Administration. These efforts were primarily driven by China's OBOR propaganda campaigns on the international stage. As shared by Xi Jinping at the Arab League in 2016 – to facilitate exchange of ideas and talents, China and the Middle East committed to engage in various cultural and academic initiatives such as the China–Arab Year, a China–Arab Research Center, the "Silk Road Book Translation" program, exchange programs for scholars, and scholarships to Arab students and artists to visit and study in China. China announced its plan to jointly translate 100 classic books into both Arabian and Chinese. China also promised to support an exchange of 100 scholars and experts annually, to provide 1,000 training opportunities for young Arab leaders, and invite 1,500 leaders of Arab political parties to visit China. Additionally, China committed to provide 10,000 scholarships and 10,000 training opportunities for Arab states and organize mutual visits for 10,000 Chinese and Arab artists in the same year. Finally, China initiated cooperation between 100 cultural institutions from both sides. By 2016, the number of students sent to China had exceed 14,000 and there are currently nearly a dozen Confucius Institutes in Arab states (CRI 2016).

With these heightened cultural exchanges emerging between China and the Middle East, a mutual understanding among the people from the two sides is growing. The public sentiment about China, however, is volatile in the Middle East. There were difficult feelings about China when Beijing supported regimes like Syria and Iran. In the Syrian case, many people took to the streets to protest against the Chinese government in the wake of China's veto of the UN resolution on Syria. In addition, the public remained skeptical about China's alleged sincerity in promoting economic development in the region (Olimat 2014). With regard to Iran, Middle East public opinion was by no means positive about the country. Despite an overall positive perception of China among the wider public in the Middle East, China's influence in the region was almost invisible in the eyes of the people of the region in comparison to the US, Russia, and Turkey as revealed in a 2017 PEW survey (Fetterolf and Poushter 2017).

Conclusion

There are prominent signs of both changes and continuities in Beijing's engagement with the Middle East under Xi Jinping's administration. It is evident that both Beijing's interests and its stakes in the Middle East have been considerably augmented since 2013 when the Middle East, ceased to be a peripheral interest. With China's soaring trade volume, heavy investment in the region, proactive diplomacy as peace mediator, expanded military interactions, as well as Beijing's keen projection of its soft power – China undoubtedly became a more visible player in the region. This heightened presence nonetheless reflects the status of the country as a newly self-conscious great power that is becoming more assertive and confident on the international stage. As China further enters into practical cooperation with Middle East countries along the OBOR route and Beijing recalibrates its foreign policy in line with its status as a great power, it is likely that Beijing's involvement in the region will deepen in the years to come.

However, China's enhanced economic, military, cultural, and diplomatic activism in the Middle East should not be exaggerated. The neutrality Beijing exercises when working with regional conflicts, its pronounced position of not finding proxies in the region, and its commitment to not align with any parties even in the antiterrorism coalition – as well as its insistence on political settlements of all regional conflicts – invariably confirmed China's intention to avoid deep entanglements in regional affairs. Instead, Beijing is more enthusiastic about promoting its own model of engaging the Middle East. China seems to hope that by promoting regional economic prosperity under the framework of the OBOR and also advocating political settlements of the region's conflicts, it will foster stability and cement its power and influence as a newly emerged great power with minimum cost. However, the OBOR will not be implemented smoothly without a proper settlement of the military conflicts in the region.

As China continues to push for its OBOR initiative, the more deeply intertwined interests between China and the region – and the rising international expectations for China thereafter – will likely push Beijing to take a more decisive stand. Beijing will have to articulate its Arab Policy and define its interests in the region much more clearly. Before this happens, Beijing is likely to continue to walk the tightrope as a wary dragon between symbolically involving itself in Middle East conflicts and simultaneously protecting its expanded economic interests in the region.

China's new grand Middle East Policy is yet to emerge. However, Beijing's friendly relations with the governments of the region, its rising international influence, and its more assertive foreign policy will – if managed well – combine to enable China to play a more substantial role in the region.

References

Arun, Swati. 2018. "China" in P.R. Kumaraswarmy and Meena Singh Roy eds., *Persian Gulf 2016–2017: Indian's Relations with the Region*. New Delhi: Pentacon Press.

Calabrese, John. 2017. "China's Role in Post Hegemonic Middle East". *Middle East Institute*. May 01, 2017. http://www.mei.edu/content/article/chinas-role-post-hegemonic-middle-east.

Chaziza, Mordechai. 2016. "China's Middle East Policy: The ISIS Factor". *Middle East Policy*, Vol. XXIII, No. 1, Spring.

Dittmer, Lowell. 2015. "China Dream, China World". In the *China Dreams: China's New Leadership and Future Impacts* edited by Chn-Shian Liou and Arthur S. Ding, *33–56*. Singapore: World Scientific Publishing Co.

Dusek, Mirek and Maroun Kairouz. 2017. "Is China Pivoting towards the Middle East?", *World Economic Forum*, April 4, 2017, https://www.weforum.org/agenda/2017/04/is-china-pivoting-towards-the-middle-east/.

Erdbrink, Thomas. 2016. "China Deepens its Footprint in Iran after Lifting of Sanctions". *The New York Times*, 24 January 2016. https://www.nytimes.com/2016/01/25/world/middleeast/china-deepens-its-footprint-in-iran-after-lifting-of-sanctions.html.

Fetterolf, Janell and Jacob Poushter. "Key Middle East Publics See Russia, Turkey and US All Playing Larger Roles in Region". Pew Research Center, December 11, 2017. http://www.pewglobal.org/2017/12/11/key-middle-east-publics-see-russia-turkey-and-u-s-all-playing-larger-roles-in-region/.

Gao, Zugui. 2015. "China-Middle East Relations since the Middle East Crisis". *Arab World Studies*, No. 1. 14–22. http://www.mesi.shisu.edu.cn/_upload/article/04/29/01adacbb411085376090ae9285d7/ca7422ce-07a4-48d7-a98a-e9a46607695f.pdf

Ghosal, Debalina. 2016. "China Pivots to the Middle East and Iran". *Yale Global Online*, July 7, 2016. https://yaleglobal.yale.edu/content/china-pivots-middle-east-and-iran.

Hayoun, Massound, 2016. "China's Approach to the Middle East Looks Familiar". *The Diplomat*, November 29. https://thediplomat.com/2016/11/chinas-approach-to-the-middle-east-looks-familiar/.

Irish, John. 2016. "China Rules out Joining Anti-Terrorism Coalitions, Says Helping Iraq". *Reuters*, February 12, 2016. https://www.reuters.com/article/us-mideast-crisis-china/china-rules-out-joining-anti-terrorism-coalitions-says-helping-iraq-idUSKCN0VL1SV.

Jin, Wang. 2016. "China and Saudi Arabia: A New Alliance?". *The Diplomat*, September 2, 2016. https://thediplomat.com/2016/09/china-and-saudi-arabia-a-new-alliance/.

Liao, Janet Xuanli. 2013. "China's Energy Diplomacy and its peaceful rise ambition: the case of Sudan and Iran". *Asian Journal of Peacebuidling*, Vol. 1, No. 2, 197–225.

Luft, Gal. "China's Grand Strategy for the Middle East". *Foreign Policy*, 26 January 2016. http://foreignpolicy.com/2016/01/26/chinas-new-middle-east-grand-strategy-iran-saudi-arabia-oil-xi-jinping/.

Ma, Xiaolin. 2010. "Chinese Media Coverage of the Middle East over the Past 60 Years." *Arab World Studies*. No. 2. 49–60. http://www.mesi.shisu.edu.cn/_upload/article/d1/8f/cd08a3cf44bcacf6e08bd5efa50b/05267127-4d1b-4bce-899f-28ec91cc2169.pdf.

Marcus, Jonathan. "The 'globalisation' of China's military power". BBC, February 13, 2018. https://www.bbc.com/news/world-asia-china-43036302.

N.D.. 2017. *Xin Jinping on Governance (Volume 2)*. Beijing: Foreign Language Publishing House.

Olimat, Muhamad. 2013. *China and the Middle East: From Silk Road to Arab Spring*. New York: Routledge.

Olimat, Muhamad S. 2014. *China and the Middle East since World War II*. New York: Rowman & Littlefied-Lexignton.

Pan, Guang. 1997. "China's Success in the Middle East", *Middle East Quarterly*, December: 35–40. https://www.meforum.org/articles/other/china-s-success-in-the-middle-east.

Perlez, Jane, "President Xi Jinping of China Is All Business in Middle East Visit". *The New York Times*, January 30, 2016. https://www.nytimes.com/2016/01/31/world/asia/xi-jinping-visits-saudi-iran.html.

Romaniuk, Scott M. and Tobias J. Burgers. 2016. "China's 'Arab Pivot' Signals the End of Non-Interference: China's Interests in the Middle East may Lead Beijing to Assure a Military Role in the Affair of Arab States." *The Diplomat*, December 20, 2016. https://thediplomat.com/2016/12/chinas-arab-pivot-signals-the-end-of-non-intervention/.

Scobell, Andrew and Alirera Nader. 2016. *China in the Middle East*. New York: Rand Corporation

Sharma, Bal Krishan and Nivedita Das Kundu. eds. 2016. *China's One Belt One Road: Intiative, Challenges, and Prospects*. New Delhi: Vij Books India Pvt Ltd.

Shicor, Yizhak. 1979. *The Middle East in China's Foreign Policy, 1947–1977*. New York: Cambridge University Press.

Simpfenforfer, Ben. 2009. *The New Silk Road: How A Rising Arab World is Turning away from the West and Rediscovering China*. New York: Palgrave Macmillan.

Su, Alice. 2016. "'Let's not Talk Politics': China Builds Middle East Ties Through Business". *Al-Jazeera America*, 20 February 2016. http://america.aljazeera.com/articles/2016/2/20/china-middle-east-business-politics.html

Vice, Margaret. "In global popularity contest, US and China – not Russia – vie for first". *Pew Research Center*, August 23, 2017. http://www.pewresearch.org/fact-tank/2017/08/23/in-global-popularity-contest-u-s-and-china-not-russia-vie-for-first/.

Wagner, Daniel and Giorgio Cafiero. "Is the US Losing Saudi Arabia to China?". *Huffington Post,* January 23, 2014. https://www.huffingtonpost.com/daniel-wagner/is-the-us-losing-saudi-ar_b_4176729.html

Xu, Qinduo. "Xi Jinping in the Middle East, Treading New Ground". *Xinhuanet*, January 24, 2016. http://www.xinhuanet.com/english/china/2016-01/20/c_135028537.htm

"Arab Policy Paper". *Xinhua*, 13 January 2016. http://www.xinhuanet.com/english/china/2016-01/13/c_135006619.htm

" Backgrounder: China-Arab States Cooperation Forum". *Xinhuanet*. May 12, 2016. http://www.xinhuanet.com/english/2016-05/12/c_135354230.htm.

"China Holds First Anti-Terror drills with Saudi Arabia". *Reuters*, October 27, 2016. http://www.reuters.com/article/us-china-saudi-security-idUSKCN12R0FD.

"China to host Palestine-Israel peace symposium". *Xinhuanet*, December 15, 2017. http://www.xinhuanet.com/english/2017-12/15/c_136829097.htm.

"China, Jerusalem and the Israeli-Palestinian Conflict". *Middle East Institute*, February 20, 2018. http://www.mei.edu/content/map/china-jerusalem-and-israeli-palestinian-conflict.

"China Seeks Support for Israel-Palestinian Peace Plan," *South China Morning Post*, August 1, 2017. http://www.scmp.com/news/china/diplomacy-defence/article/2104968/china-seeks-support-israel-palestinian-peace-plan.

"China Issues Arab Policy Paper". *State Council, The People's Republic of China*, January 13, 2016. http://english.gov.cn/news/international_exchanges/2016/01/13/content_281475271410542.htm

"China Surpassed the United States as the World's Largest Crude Oil Importer in 2017". *EIA*, February 5, 2018. https://www.eia.gov/todayinenergy/detail.php?id=34812.

"China and Iran Carry out Naval Exercise near Strait of Hormuz as US Holds Drill with Qatar". *South China Morning Post*, June 19, 2017. http://www.scmp.com/news/china/diplomacy-defence/article/2098898/china-and-iran-carry-out-naval-exercise-near-strait.

Foreign Ministry Spokesperson Hong Lei's Remarks on the UN Security Council's Vote on the Draft Resolution to Refer the Situation in Syria to the International Criminal Court. *Ministry of Foreign Affairs (FMPRC)*, May 23, 2014. http://www.fmprc.gov.cn/mfa_eng/xwfw_665399/s2510_665401/2535_665405/t1158923.shtml.

"News Analysis: Belt & Road Initiative shores up China-Mideast cooperation". *Xinhuanet*, January 23, 2016. http://www.xinhuanet.com/english/2016-01/23/c_135038752.htm.

"Palestine-Israel Peace Symposium: Two State Solution only Viable Option". *Xinhuanet*, December 23, 2017. http://www.xinhuanet.com/english/2017-12/23/c_136846269.htm.

"Special Envoy of the Chinese Government on Syrian Issue Xie Xiaoyan Attends Geneva Peace Talks on Syrian Issue". *Foreign Ministry of the People's Republic of China (FMPRC)*, March 28, 2017. http://www.fmprc.gov.cn/mfa_eng/wjb_663304/zzjg_663340/xybfs_663590/xwlb_663592/t1450517.shtml.

"Special Envoy of the Chinese Government on Syrian Issue Xie Xiaoyan Visits Syria". *FMPRC*, June 18, 2017. http://www.fmprc.gov.cn/mfa_eng/wjb_663304/zzjg_663340/xybfs_663590/xwlb_663592/t1472117.shtml.

"Special Envoy of the Chinese Government on Syrian Issue Xie Xiaoyan Visits Egypt". FMPRC, April 24, 2017. http://www.fmprc.gov.cn/mfa_eng/wjb_663304/zzjg_663340/xybfs_663590/xwlb_663592/t1457302.shtml.

"The Great Well of China, Economists". *The Economist*, June 20, 2015. https://www.economist.com/middle-east-and-africa/2015/06/18/the-great-well-of-china.

"China's Xi says to prioritize energy cooperation with Iran", *Reuters*, September 29, 2015. https://ca.reuters.com/article/topNews/idCAKCN0RT0B920150929.

"China, Iraq sign memo to promote energy partnership". *State Council of the People's Republic of China*, December 23, 2015. http://english.gov.cn/premier/news/2015/12/23/content_281475259135066.htm.

"New Analysis: Belt and Road Initiative Shores up China-Mideast Cooperation". *Xinhuanet*, January 23, 2016. http://www.xinhuanet.com/english/2016-01/23/c_135038752.htm.

"Work Together for a Bright Future of China-Arab Relations" (Chinese President Xi Jinping's Speech at the Arab League Headquarter). January 21, 2016. http://english.cri.cn/12394/2016/01/22/4182s914033.htm.

"The Middle East's Pivot to Asia". *Foreign Policy*, April 24, 2015. http://foreignpolicy.com/2015/04/24/the-middle-easts-pivot-to-asia-china/.

"Xi's Fruitful Middle East Tour Highlights China's Commitment to Building New Type of Int'l Relations". *Xinhuanet*, January 24, 2016. http://www.xinhuanet.com/english/2016-01/24/c_135040319.htm.

"President Xi Jinping Visits Saudi Arabia, Egypt, Iran". *Xinhuanet*. http://www.xinhuanet.com/english/cnleaders/201601xjp/index.htm.

"China's Xi Calls for Greater Counter-Terrorism Cooperation with Turkey". *Reuters*, May 13, 2017. https://www.reuters.com/article/us-china-silkroad-turkey/chinas-xi-calls-for-greater-counter-terrorism-cooperation-with-turkey-idUSKBN18A01D.

"Dont Expect 'Quick Fix' in Syria, China Tells EU". *EUObserver*, April 26, 2017. https://euobserver.com/foreign/137680.

"China Adopts First Counter-Terrorism Law in History". *Xinhuanet*, December 27, 2015. http://www.xinhuanet.com/english/2015-12/27/c_134956054.htm.

6

The EU and the Middle East: From the Euro-Mediterranean Partnership to the Union for the Mediterranean

STEFANIE GEORGAKIS ABBOTT

Europe has a complex history with its Middle Eastern and North African (MENA) neighbors. From colonial histories to a unified policy agenda, Europe has long sought to expand its sphere of influence to the Middle East and North Africa. European history, and certainly the history of the European Union as a political project, is inextricable from its policies towards its immediate neighbors around the Mediterranean. While Europe's historical relationship with its MENA neighbors is largely built on colonialism, it was not until fairly recently that the EU created a formal, unified policy towards its MENA neighbors. The development of European policy during the Cold War marked a shift towards addressing "Mediterranean security in a regional and multilateral framework" (Del Sarto 2006, 10). It wasn't until the 1990s that the MENA region took a sharper focus in EU foreign policy concerns. Attached to this focus was a prolific language of security and stability in the region (Kienle 1998; Romeo 1998). As the Soviet Union collapsed, the geopolitics of the region shifted focus and Europe began to expand its influence in its Mediterranean neighborhood. Increasingly, issues such as immigration, terrorism, trafficking, and energy needs shifted European attention to the southern and eastern parts of the Mediterranean.

Since 1995, the region has taken on further importance for the EU, both within the foreign policy and domestic arenas. The EU states that its MENA neighbors represent the intersection of "strategic" or "practical" concerns for the EU and speak to its significant contribution throughout history to "the mutual enrichment of cultures and civilizations" (Commission of the European Communities 2003a, 13). By the mid-2000s, the existing Euro-Mediterranean relationships became defined institutionally through two pillars: the European Neighborhood Policy and the Union for the Mediterranean (including its predecessors). By engaging in the maintenance of economic, political, and humanitarian security in the region, the EU's proactive foreign policy towards its Middle Eastern and North African neighbors has two main objectives: to encourage political and economic reform in MENA countries and to ensure regional cooperation between the EU and its neighbors. Broadly speaking, the EU's current policy towards the MENA region focuses on three strategies. First, the EU seeks to encourage and facilitate political, social, humanitarian, and economic reform in its MENA neighbors. Second, the EU seeks to deepen relationships, both bilaterally and regionally, between the EU and its non-European partners as well as between MENA states themselves. Third, a significant amount of the EU's attention towards the region has focused on Israeli–Palestinian relations.

The goal of this chapter is to trace the origin and trajectory of the Union for the Mediterranean, including its antecedents, namely the Euro-Mediterranean Partnership (Barcelona Process).

The Barcelona Process: Towards a More Formalized Relationship with the South

The Barcelona Process, which came to include the Euro-Mediterranean Partnership (EMP) and the Union for the Mediterranean (UfM), was created under the auspices of trying to ameliorate relations and mitigate inequality between the EU and its southern and southeastern neighbors. The Barcelona Declaration was signed in 1995 and institutionalized the partnership between the EU and its southern Mediterranean neighbors. The Barcelona process led to the creation of the Euro-Mediterranean Partnership (EMP), demonstrating the attempts on the part of the EU to create a unified and defined foreign policy towards the region. It was seen as a way to augment the strategic relationships between the EU and the southern states in the European Neighbourhood Policy. The European Union outlines the institutional importance of the MENA region, noting that the Barcelona Process improves the relationship between the EU and MENA by:

1. Upgrading the political level of the EU's relationship with its Mediterranean partners;
2. Providing for further co-ownership to our multilateral relations; and;
3. Making these relations more concrete and visible through additional regional and sub- regional projects, relevant for the citizens of the region

(Secretariat of the Union for the Mediterranean 2008a, 13).

The formation of an institutionalized relationship between the EU and the MENA states was influenced by discourses of pragmatism and strategy – that the Mediterranean region was strategically a good place for Europe to invest its economic and political resources. Similarly, the Paris Summit, which reemphasized the importance of a European policy towards the MENA states, underlined the strategic importance of the region for the EU, stating:

> The Barcelona Process has been the central instrument for Euro-Mediterranean relations. Representing a partnership of 39 governments and over 700 million people, it has provided a framework for continued engagement and development. The Barcelona Process is the only forum within which all Euro-Mediterranean partners exchange views and engage in constructive dialogue. It represents a strong commitment to peace, democracy, regional stability and security through regional cooperation and integration (Secretariat of the Union for the Mediterranean 2008a, 8).

The Paris Summit emphasized the goals of the EU's policy in the region towards pursuing a "mutually and effectively verifiable Middle East Zone free of weapons of mass destruction, nuclear, chemical and biological, and their delivery systems" (Secretariat of the Union for the Mediterranean 2008a, 10). The Barcelona Process and the Paris Summit paved the way for decades of policy making towards the MENA region.

At the time of the initial 1995 meeting, 14 non-EU member states were included in the conference. At its conception, the EMP included the fifteen EU member states, which expanded to include all 27 member-states, as well as the Mediterranean partners including Algeria, Croatia, Cyprus, Egypt, Israel, Jordan, Lebanon, Malta, Mauritania, Morocco, Syria, Tunisia, Turkey, and the Palestinian territories. Libya was added as an observer, given the EU's belief that Libya's role in the Mediterranean region could "positively contribute to the strengthening of the Euro-Mediterranean cooperation *(sic)*" (Commission of the European Communities 2003a, 4).

The Barcelona Declaration was designed with the expressed intent of uniting the two shores of the Mediterranean, creating an "area of dialogue, exchange and cooperation guaranteeing peace, stability and prosperity" (European Commission 2000a, 2). There is a direct recognition that an important aspect of this partnership is "an attempt to extend southwards the zone of peace and prosperity achieved within the EU, through a process of North–South integration" (European Commission 2005b, 4). In its five-year assessment, the European Commission noted that the Barcelona Declaration had paved the way for a partnership that intended to demonstrate an increased commitment towards equality with the southern neighbors, and that therefore the Barcelona Process should be considered "a proximity policy" (European Commission 2000). Despite making noted achievements the Commission also recognized that "the Middle East peace process [had] run into difficulties and affected the general Barcelona Process; progress with the association agreements [had] been slower than expected [and] trade among the partners themselves [was] very low" (European Commission 2000, 2).

The Euro-Mediterranean Partnership

The Euro-Mediterranean Partnership was originally organized into three categories, or pillars, focusing on political stability, economic prosperity, and social cooperation for the states on the southern and eastern shores of the Mediterranean. In 2005, a fourth focus area – migration – was also added. The fourth basket was meant to address concerns on the part of some EU member that immigration originating from the MENA region is threatening the security of EU member states.

The Euro-Mediterranean Partnership has the stated long-term goal, which in many ways has been achieved, of "turning [the] Mediterranean basin into an area of dialogue, exchange and cooperation guaranteeing peace, stability and prosperity" (Council of the European Union 1995).

Political and Security Basket

The first pillar of the Barcelona Process, "Political & security partnership: Establishing a common area of peace and stability," focuses on the development of political stability and security with an emphasis on 'good governance' practices, the development of democratic regimes, and the protection of human rights (Council of the European Union 1995). Specifically, the EMP focuses the first basket on three complementary parts. There is a desire to:

1. Increase political dialogue on both bilateral and regional level[s];
2. Ensure partnership-building measures;
3. Develop the Charter for Peace and Stability, which was meant to help identify areas of friction and disagreement in the Mediterranean (European Commission 2000).

These parts constitute the largest of the objectives of the EMP. Political integration of states to the south of the EU works to increase interdependence and reduce the inequalities expressed across the Mediterranean, while stopping short of political integration into the EU. While the political basket focuses on securitizing the MENA region, it highlights the ambiguity of the EU's relationship with its southern border. The political and security basket provides a logic to monitor and manage political developments in the southern Mediterranean states, and sets up a "code of conduct" for the area (Council of the European Union 1995).

Despite the attention and resources dedicated to developing democratic institutions and political reform in southern and eastern Mediterranean states, it has been argued that "in practice Mediterranean governments were hostile to funding encroaching upon the political sphere" (Youngs 2001, 86). The structure of the Euro-Mediterranean Partnership specifically nested discussions of political reform and the promotion of democratic governance with issues of economic development, thus speaking to the role of discourses of democratization in the EU's foreign policy creation. As Youngs notes, during the 1990s the European Union launched a set of narratives which linked democratization, economic development, and strategic interests in external states (Youngs 2001, 13). The political basket of the EMP, moreover, has perhaps been the least "successful" in terms of achieving stated goals, and has resulted in tensions over the goals of democratization on the part of the EU in the Mediterranean.

Economic and Financial Basket

The second pillar, "Economic & financial partnership: Creating an area of shared prosperity," emphasizes the purported importance of "sustainable and balanced economic development of the countries of the Mediterranean region" (Council of the European Union 1995). Within the second chapter, the EMP notes three interconnected objectives:

> The establishment of a Euro-Mediterranean free trade area, EU support for economic transition and to help the partners meet the challenges posed by economic liberalization, and the increase of investment flows to the Mediterranean partners which will result from a tree trade and economic liberalization (European Commission 2000, 10).

This pillar expresses a primary interest in mitigating poverty and lower life expectancy in non-European Mediterranean states, such as Morocco, Algeria, Tunisia, and Egypt, through an emphasis on development and the creation of a Mediterranean free trade zone (Council of the European Union 1995;

Philippart 2003, 210). With the adoption of the EMP, a large number of free trade agreements were signed bilaterally between states, although the project of a "region-wide" free-trade area has largely failed (Handoussa and Reiffers 2001). Accordingly, the fight against poverty is a stated goal of the EMP, particularly as the per capita income in the EU is about ten times higher than in the Mediterranean partners (Noi 2011, 39).

Another dimension of the economic basket is the development of free trade areas. The establishment of the free trade area in the Mediterranean, despite a significant amount of emphasis placed on economic integration by the EMP, is largely seen as a failure. In 2000, however, intraregional trade only accounted for "5% of the 12 Mediterranean partners' trade volume" while only "a mere 2% of European FDI flow[s] into the Mediterranean region" (European Commission 2000, 13). As the EU notes, even after its inception, the Free Trade Area did not guarantee greater access to the internal markets of the EU to the Mediterranean partners, but rather focused on the creation of "horizontal exchange of goods, capital and human resources [with the intent of] creat[ing] markets large enough to attract significant foreign direct investment, which in turn are indispensable for sustainable economic growth" (European Commission 2000, 11). The financial basket of the EMP emphasizes the economic interconnectedness of the EU and its Mediterranean neighbors. More importantly, it positions "free trade [not as] an end in itself, but rather a means to a much bigger goal: the creation of a stable, peaceful and prosperous Mediterranean" (European Commission 2000, 12).

The principal financial instrument for implementing the economic efforts of the EMP is the *Mesure d'Accompagnement* (MEDA) program and was adopted by the Council in July of 1996. The MEDA program provides a structure through which economic and financial initiatives can be carried out, increasing the interdependence between the EU and its southern Mediterranean partners (Philippart 2001). However, in 2007 MEDA was replaced with a financial instrument of the European Neighborhood Policy (ENP), the European Neighborhood and Partnership Instrument (ENPI). Between 2007 and 2013, the program has an estimated 12-billion-euro budget for assistance given to the southern and eastern Mediterranean states (Commission of the European Communities 2008; Noi 2011).

It remains to be seen whether or not initiatives undertaken through this pillar are beneficial to the citizens of the non-European Mediterranean states. After five years of the implementation of the EMP, the "per capita income in the EU [was still] approximately 10 times higher than that of the Mediterranean partners" (European Commission 2000, 13), while the:

Combined gross domestic product of the Maghreb States (Algeria, Morocco, Tunisia; population: 66 million) is less than that of Portugal (populations: 10 million), while the GDP of the Mashreq States (Jordan, Egypt, Lebanon, Syria; population: 86 million) roughly equals that of Greece or Finland (population: 10 and 5 million respectively) (European Commission 2000, 13).

Social, Cultural, and Human Basket

The third pillar outlines the goals for the EMP with regards to the social and culture objectives. The main objective of this basket is to promote intercultural dialogue, particularly through an emphasis on shared culture between the northern and southern shores of the Mediterranean. The Barcelona Declaration specifically states that the partnership seeks to increase the role of mass media; develop training programs for young people in the area of human resources; improve health and well-being among populations; to establish closer cooperation between states with regards to the problem of irregular migration; and to fight against drug and human trafficking, to name a few (Council of the European Union 1995). It is acknowledged in this portion of the Barcelona Declaration that the area of human resources and intercultural awareness cannot be divorced from the aims of economic development, and thus the "human" aspect of the Barcelona Declaration becomes important.

This pillar has arguably been the most successful in achieving its goals. The EMP noted during its five and ten-year reviews that the three main projects undertaken by the cultural and social basket have had the most profound impact. These objectives are the development of three particular programs:

1. Euromed Heritage: for the preservation and development of Euro-Mediterranean cultural heritage. The success of this initiative has encouraged the EU to launch a second phase in 2000.
2. Euromed Audiovisual: supporting Euro-Mediterranean audiovisual cooperation projects in the field of radio, television and cinema.
3. Euromed Youth: in the field of youth exchange aiming at facilitating the integration of young people into social and professional life and stimulating the democratization of the civil society of the Mediterranean partners in that it improves mutual comprehension and cohesion between young people across the Mediterranean basin (European Commission 2000, 15).

After September 11, 2001, the states' aims of the cultural basket became more emphasized, especially as the cultural aspects of the partnership were brought to the fore in discussions of the "incompatibility" of predominantly Muslim cultures in Europe (M. Pace 2006, 117). The EU notes that "one of the main obstacles to the further development of the Barcelona Process has been the inability, on both shores of the Mediterranean, to deal with the growing political significance of Islamist forces in Southern countries" (European Union Institute for Security Studies 2008, 16). While programs launched under this basket include a Euro-Mediterranean University and other youth programs designed to increase intercultural dialogue and understanding and to overcome the challenges of xenophobia, the language used in the articulation of this basket and its objectives is dubious.

New Objectives: The Fourth Basket

In 2005, a fourth pillar was added to the EMP, with a specific focus on immigration (Portugal Presidency of the European Union 2007; Council of the European Union 2005). Although immigration is mentioned as an area for attention in all three of the other pillars, it became a large enough concern to warrant more concentration and is perhaps one of the most resonant of the EU's security concerns (Youngs 2001, 57). For example, in the original Barcelona Declaration, the third pillar placed emphasis on the fact that the partners recognize the "importance of the role played by migration in their relationships" (Council of the European Union 1995, 6).

Specifically, this new pillar places a large emphasis on ways to create legal pathways to migration between the EU and other Mediterranean countries, finding ways to avoid brain drain, and promoting "sustainable return of migrants to their countries of origin" (Noi 2011, 44; Portugal Presidency of the European Union 2007, 2). Within the EMP framework, two major migration-based initiatives have been undertaken, with a combined budget of 7 million Euros (Noi 2011, 45). These two programs, entitled Euro-Med Migration I and II, work to create focus groups between the EU and non-member Mediterranean states to tackle the proposed need for legislative convergence and reform of migration laws in Partnership states.

The projected scope of the EMP involved a dense network of institutions and programs between the EU and its southern neighbors, the partnership aspect of the Barcelona Process is in effect one of the weakest elements (R. Joffé 1996; Del Sarto 2006). On one hand, in 1999 the Commission noted "three and half years after the inaugural conference in Barcelona, the Euro-Mediterranean Partnership has developed and strengthened considerably and has given clear proof of its viability in sometimes delicate and difficult circumstances" (Commission of the European Communities 1999). Yet by 2003, almost ten years after the launching of the project, political reform in southern Partner states did not meet the EU's expectations and the European Commission noted that "political reform in the majority of the countries of the Mediterranean has not progressed as quickly as desired" (Commission of the European Communities 2003b, 7). Furthermore, despite these mixed reviews on the part of the EU itself, the proposed Free Trade Area was not established by 2010, and there has arguably been "a worsening state of human development" in the region (Wolff 2012, 5). As Benita Ferrero-Waldner notes in the Barcelona process's ten-year review, the EMP had until 2005 functioned more as an inter-governmental process and acknowledged that the organization needed to better address "questions that are of the interest of the citizens and should be at the center of [the] concerns in the partnership" (European Commission 2005, 1).

Among the southern partners, a lack of cooperation and development on the political front, particularly amongst Israel and the Arab states of Jordan, Syria, and Egypt has contributed to the failures in the economic front. Thus, many of the attempts to create multilateral talks stalled, which left the European Union created bilateral agreements with individual countries in the south (Vasconcelos and Joffé 2004, 4). The view of the project as mainly an economic one has highlighted the lack of political dialogue between southern partners themselves, as well as within north–south discussions, leading some to conclude that the political basket has perhaps been the largest shortcoming (M. Pace 2006; Commission of the European Communities 2003a; Vasconcelos and Joffé 2004). The EU acknowledged that "a reinvigorated cooperation within the region and with Mediterranean partners should be sought" (Commission of the European Communities 2003), again emphasizing the political and strategic importance of the region for the EU.

Returning to Barcelona in November of 2005 to celebrate the tenth anniversary of the Declaration, the Euro-Mediterranean Heads of State and Government met for the first time in a decade. While a five-year work program was released that reiterated many of the same commitments that the Barcelona Declaration had a decade earlier, the Summit brought attention to the dysfunction of the Partnership, as Palestinian President Mahmoud Abbas and then Turkish Prime Minister Recep Erdoğan were the only representatives of the non-European Mediterranean countries that were in attendance (Council of the European Union 2005; Youngs and Kausch 2009).

The boycott of the Arab states at the 2005 Euro–Mediterranean Summit, along with the disappointing progress towards political and economic reforms and dialogue in the region led some to write the Partnership off, or at the very least allowed many academics and analysts to largely ignore any evaluation or explanation of the EU policies in the region (S. Wolff 2012, 5). However, despite its lack of success in terms of its stated goals, the EMP is largely important and significant for developing an understanding of the EU's persistence towards trying to establish a meaning of the Mediterranean, in order to articulate a coherent policy towards the region. As Wolff notes, much of the literature on the EMP has focused on the political failures and has lacked any in depth discussion of the symbolic importance of the Partnership, failing to question "the dynamics at hand behind the EU's governance in the Mediterranean" (S. Wolff 2012, 5). Others have argued that at the end of the day, the Barcelona Process and the EMP remains a neo-colonial mechanism which reinforces "a Eurocentric and dichotomist framework where true dialogue cannot flourish" (M. Pace and Schumacher 2004, 124). Clearly, there remains a large disparity between the southern and northern Mediterranean.

The Union for the Mediterranean

In light of the dubious acceptance of the EMP, in 2008 it was relaunched and shifted to form the Union of the Mediterranean (UfM). The UfM was inspired not solely through the revamping of the EMP, but was also influenced by a proposal on the part of former French President Nicolas Sarkozy, who envisioned a more institutionally integrated, formal union for the northern and southern Mediterranean countries. Sarkozy made his vision for an integrated Mediterranean Union clear during his acceptance speech after winning the 2007 presidential election:

> I want to issue a call to all the people of the Mediterranean to tell them that it is in the Mediterranean that everything is going to be played out, that we have to overcome all kinds of hatred to pave the way for a great dream of peace and a great dream of civilization. I want to tell them that the time has come to build together a Mediterranean union that will form a link between Europe and Africa ("Nicolas Sarkozy: Victory Speech Excerpts" 2007).

The Union for the Mediterranean launched in 2008 and Sarkozy added "we had dreamt of it. The Union for the Mediterranean is now a reality" (Vucheva 2008).

Although initially facing skepticism from European leaders, namely German Chancellor Angela Merkel who warned of the development of "a Europe of private functions" (EurActiv 2012), the Union for the Mediterranean was created by the 42 Euro–Mediterranean Partners' Heads of State and Government on July 13, 2008 at a summit in Paris. The headquarters remained in Barcelona, as the UfM was meant to build upon the statues and goals of the Barcelona Process and the EMP. According to the UfM, the representatives at the Paris Summit demonstrated the shared:

> Conviction that this initiative can play an important role in addressing common challenges facing the Euro-Mediterranean region, such as economic and social development; world food security crisis; degradation of the environment, including climate change and desertification, with the view of promoting sustainable development; energy; migration; terrorism and extremism; as well as promoting dialogue between cultures (Secretariat of the Union for the Mediterranean 2008, 8).

In March of 2008, the European Council approved the idea of a Union for the Mediterranean, agreeing to call it "Barcelona Process: Union for the Mediterranean" (Commission of the European Communities 2008). The UfM is seen as a way for the urgency of the common challenges that Europe and the Mediterranean face to be revisited and given greater political importance (Commission of the European Communities 2008).

The UfM expanded the states included in the Barcelona Process, and now includes 43 members, including all EU member states, as well as Morocco, Algeria, Egypt, Tunisia, Israel, Mauritania, Albania, Lebanon, Jordan, Syria, Turkey, and the Palestinian territories. The UfM also added Monaco, Croatia, Bosnia and Herzegovina, and Montenegro to the partnership, noting that these states "have accepted the *acquis* of the Barcelona Process" (Secretariat of the Union for the Mediterranean 2008a, 8).

Rather than replacing the structure of the EMP, the UfM was meant to build upon the EMP, filling in any areas of weakness and leading to a further regimentation of the Mediterranean area (Secretariat of the Union for the Mediterranean 2008a). The introduction to the statutes clearly display this:

> The participants at the Paris Summit for the Mediterranean on 13 July 2008 agreed that the Union for the Mediterranean (UfM) will build on the Barcelona Declaration of 28 November 1995, promote its goals...and further reinforce the *acquis* of the Barcelona Process by upgrading their relations, incorporating more co-ownership in their multilateral cooperation framework, strengthening equal footing governance and translate it into concrete projects, thus delivering concrete

benefits for the citizens of the region (Secretariat of the Union for the Mediterranean 2008b, 1).

The statutes also outlined the need to:

> establish new institutional structures to contribute to achieving the political goals of the initiative *inter alia* through the setting up of a Secretariat with a key role within the institutional architecture of the UfM (Secretariat of the Union for the Mediterranean 2008b, 1).

The Secretariat allowed for a more formalized relationship between the EU and its Mediterranean partners by introducing a secretary general and deputy secretary general and focusing on increasing monitoring of projects funded and conducted by the UfM. Furthermore, the UfM came with a stated interest in "increasing regional integration and cohesion" (Secretariat of the Union for the Mediterranean 2008a, 8).

A decision was taken to establish bi-annual summits to "enhance the visibility of the Barcelona Process" (Gillespie 2008, 281). The new forum differed from the EMP, which used conferences of foreign ministers of each state to come to decisions regarding the partnership (Commission of the European Communities 2008; Secretariat of the Union for the Mediterranean 2008b). Thus, as the EU notes, this change was meant to provide more co-ownership to the multilateral relationships formed through the Barcelona Process (Commission of the European Communities 2008; Balfour 2009, 102). This shift is significant given the criticism that the EMP received for lacking a substantial movement towards political "partnership" between the EU and its southern neighbors.

The Arab Spring and the Future of the EU–Mediterranean Relations

The wave of uprisings and revolutions across the Arab world post 2010 (popularly known as the Arab Spring) should not have caught anyone by surprise. The rampant inequality and political oppression in many countries across the MENA region, exacerbated by the demographic reality of populations whose citizens were largely both unemployed and under the age of 25, created a political and social tinderbox. Yet in the wake of the Arab Spring, we should ask what role the EU played in exacerbating, or at the very least failing to mitigate, the circumstances that created the momentum for the Arab Spring. Is it an indication that the Barcelona Process's focus on creating incentives for economic, social, and political reform failed? Or does it constitute a missed opportunity for the EU in the region? Understandably, the

EU's involvement in formal partnerships in the region, and the expressed focus on political reform, human rights, and democracy for its MENA neighbors was misaligned with the reality of political oppression, "rigged" elections, and declining living standards across the region.

One reality of the EU's relationship with its MENA neighbors is that the focus on economic issues has largely been on a state-to-state level. As a result, there is the fair perception that many of the EU's initiatives are Janus faced. In addition to the perceived failure to foresee the Arab Spring, there is also a question of how genuine and effective the EU's response to the Arab Spring was, or whether it was too little, too late (Etzioni 2011). In the years since the Arab Spring uprisings, many Arab populations across the region are still under dire political and economic constraints. There is an opportunity for a renewed cooperation and a recommitment to democracy and economic development in the region.

Conclusion

What does the future hold for these strategic partnerships between the EU and the MENA region? In a region that is marred by political instability, it is hard to see where European policies towards MENA states go from here. The complications, both from within the EU and from the MENA states, make it difficult to see how these political, institutional instruments for encouraging stability can accomplish their stated goals.

In November of 2015, while marking the 20th anniversary of the Barcelona Declaration, several foreign ministers from UfM countries renewed their commitment to the UfM and regional cooperation among the EU and MENA states. Yet while the members of the UfM are assuring their support of the EU's efforts in the region and the goal of coordinated cooperation, there are some concerning developments both within the EU and outside that will challenge the viability of the EU's policy and tools in the region.

Within the EU, the shockwave of the Brexit vote, as well as other waves of populist sentiment in France, Hungary, and beyond, cast doubt upon the ability of the EU to maintain a cohesive policy towards the region. While the sentiments that led to the Brexit vote went largely underestimated, they are not divorced from the external factors from the MENA region.

The regional instability created by the civil war in Syria and the refugees that the conflict has produced have created political questions within Europe about the EU's policies toward the MENA region. The refugees of the Syrian war put a massive burden on other countries in the region, like Jordan, and further disrupt European attempts to consolidation cooperation in the region. Similarly, recent developments in Turkey – including the contested results of the plebiscite that have allowed Turkish President Erdogan to consolidate his power – make it hard to imagine that just a few years ago, Turkey was in active negotiations pursuing EU membership.

Despite numerous challenges and difficulties in the region, the EU remains committed to asserting its influence on the MENA region. Increasingly though, the EU's own security depends on what happens in its "sphere of influence." Nevertheless, many European member states have long and complex histories with MENA states. The success or failure of European policy in the area might depend on contemporary factors, but one thing remains clear: it is in the EU's best interest to have a safe and secure MENA region.

References

Balfour, Rosa. 2009. "The Transformation of the Union for the Mediterranean." *Mediterranean Politics* 14 (1): 99–105.

Commission of the European Communities. 1995. "Strengthening the Mediterranean Policy of the European Union: Proposals for Implementing a Euro-Mediterranean Partnership". COM (1995) 72 final.

Commission of the European Communities. 1999. "Third Euro-Mediterranean Conference of Foreign Ministers: Chairman's Formal Conclusions."

Commission of the European Communities. 2003a. "Mid-term Euro-Mediterranean Conference: Presidency Conclusion"

Commission of the European Communities. 2003b. "Wider Europe - Neighbourhood: A New Framework for Relations with Out Eastern and Southern Neighbors". COM (2003) 104 final.

Commission of the European Communities. 2008. "Barcelona Process: Union for the Mediterranean". COM (2008) 319 final.

Council of the European Union. 1995. "Barcelona Declaration."

Council of the European Union. 2005. "10th Anniversary Euro-Mediterranean Summit: Five Year Work Programme". 15074/05 (Presse 327).

Del Sarto, Raffaela. 2006. *Contested State Identities and Regional Security in the Euro-Mediterranean Area*. New York, NY: Palgrave Macmillan.

Emerson, Michael. 2008. "CEPS Policy Brief: Making Sense of Sarkozy's Union for the Mediterranean". Centre for European Policy Studies.

European Commission. 2011. "A Dialogue for Migration, Mobility and Security with the Southern Mediterranean Countries". COM (2011) 292 final.

European Commission. 2000. "Reinvigorating the Barcelona Process". COM (2000) 497 final.

European Union Institute for Security Studies. 2008. "Union for the Mediterranean: Building on the Barcelona Acquis". Paris.

European Commission. 2005. "2005 Year of the Mediterranean: The Barcelona Process: Ten Year.

European Commission. 2003. "The Barcelona Process, Five Years on – 1995–2000". Office for Official Publications of the European Communities.

Etzioni, Amitai. "Libya: The Lost War". *The National Interest*. June 24, 2011.

Gillespie, Richard. 2008. "A 'Union for the Mediterranean' ...or for the EU?" *Mediterranean Politics* 13 (2): 277–86.

Joffé, Robert. 1996. "Integration or Peripheral Dependence: The Dilemma Facing the South Mediterranean States." In *Co-operation and Security in the Mediterranean: Prospects After Barcelona*, edited by A. Bin, 175–97. Malta: The Mediterranean Academy of Diplomatic Studies.

Kienle, Eberhard. 1998. "Destabilization Through Partnerships?: Euro-Mediterranean Relations after the Barcelona Declaration." *Mediterranean Politics* 3 (2): 1–20.

Handoussa, Heba, and J.L. Reiffers. 2001. "The FEMISE Report on the Evolution of the Structure of Trade and Investments Between the European Union and Its Mediterranean Partners". FEMISE Network.

"Nicolas Sarkozy: Victory Speech Excerpts." 2007. *BBC*, May 6. http://news.bbc.co.uk/2/hi/6631125.stm.

Noi, Aylin Unver. 2011. *The Euro-Mediterranean Partnership and the Broader Middle East and North Africa Initiative*. Lanham, MD: University Press of America, Inc.

Pace, Michelle. 2006. *The Politics of Regional Identity: Meddling with the Mediterranean*. New York: Routledge.

Pace, Michelle, and Tobias Schumacher. 2004. "Culture and Community in the Euro-Mediterranean Partnership: A Roundtable on the Third Basket, Alexandria 5-7 October 2003." *Mediterranean Politics* 9 (1): 122–26.

Pace, Roderick, and Stelios Stavridis. "The Euro-Mediterranean Parliamentary Assembly, 2004-2008: Assessing the First Years of the Parliamentary Dimension of the Barcelona Process." *Mediterranean Quarterly* 21 (2): 90–113.

Philippart, Eric. 2003. "The Euro-Mediterranean Partnership: A Critical Evaluation of an Ambitious Scheme." *European Foreign Affairs Review* 8: 201–20.

Portugal Presidency of the European Union. 2007. "First Euro-Mediterranean Ministerial Meeting on Migration (Algarve: 18, 19 November 2007) Agreed Ministerial Conclusions."

Romeo, Isabel. 1998. "The European Union and North Africa: Keeping the Mediterranean 'Safe' for Europe." *Mediterranean Politics* 3 (2): 21–38.

Secretariat of the Union for the Mediterranean. 2008a. "Joint Declaration of the Paris Summit for the Mediterranean."

Secretariat of the Union for the Mediterranean. 2008b. "Statutes of the Secretariat of the Union for the Mediterranean."

Vasconcelos, Alvaro, and George Joffé. 2004. "Towards Euro-Mediterranean Regional Integration." *Mediterranean Politics, Special Issue on the Barcelona Process. Building a Euro-Mediterranean Regional Community* 5 (1): 3–6.

Wolffe, Sarah. 2012. *The Mediterranean Dimension of the European Union's Internal Security*. New York: Palgrave Macmillan.

Youngs, Richard. 2001. *The European Union and the Promotion of Democracy: Europe's Mediterranean and Asian Politics*. New York: Oxford University Press.

Youngs, Richard, and Kristina Kausch. 2009. "The End of the 'Euro-Mediterranean Vision'." *International Affairs* 85 (5): 963–75.

7

The EU and the Middle East: The European Neighborhood Policy (ENP)

YANNIS A. STIVACHTIS

The purpose of this chapter is to provide an overview of the relations between the European Union (EU) and the countries of the Middle East and North Africa (MENA) within the framework of the European Neighborhood Policy (ENP). In doing so, the chapter is divided into four sections. The first section identifies the conditions that led to ENP's adoption, while the second section examines the ENP's contents and instruments and explores the policy's shortcomings that led to its 2011 Review. The third section focuses on the contents and instruments of the revised ENP and discusses the reasons that led to its 2015 Review. The last section focuses on the results of the 2015 Review, while some preliminary findings of the ENP's implementation are discussed in the concluding part of the chapter.

The ENP includes countries that are subdivided into two partnerships. The Eastern Partnership consists of states that were previously part of the Soviet Union (Armenia, Azerbaijan, Belarus, Georgia Moldova, and Ukraine), while the South Partnership includes countries of the MENA region (Algeria, Morocco, Egypt, Israel, Jordan, Lebanon, Libya, Syria, Tunisia, and the Palestinian Authority). In this chapter, references to the ENP would apply solely to the MENA countries.

From the Euro–Mediterranean Partnership to the European Neighborhood Policy

A number of reasons forced the EU to adopt the ENP in 2004. First, the collapse of the Middle East Peace Process led to the new Intifada and the worsening of Israeli–Palestinian/Arab relations. This development in conjunction with the 9/11 attacks that led first to the decision of the George W. Bush Administration to declare the "War on Terror" and the subsequent military intervention of the United States (US) in Afghanistan (2001) and Iraq (2003) changed the geo-strategic environment in the EU's neighborhood. Second, as a result of the 2004 EU enlargement, the external borders of the Union changed, and new security challenges emerged in the EU's "near abroad" as a consequence. Third, the results of the Euro-Mediterranean Partnership (EMP) that was introduced in 1995 were disappointing. Specifically, the EU's hesitant Common Foreign and Security Policy (CFSP) in conjunction with the conflicting views and priorities of the EU Member States had a negative impact on security-related matters in the MENA region. In addition, the EMP contribution to intercultural dialogue did not prevent the significant rise of Islamophobia in Europe, while efforts to encourage political and economic reform in MENA countries did not produce the expected results.

Although the EMP's main objective was the establishment of a free trade zone in the MENA region through economic liberalization, the real concern of the EU was about insecurity in its Southern flank and the irregular migration flows. As Malcolm Rifkind, the then British Foreign Secretary, noted: "one of the most important ways in which we can achieve political security is economic growth" and that "political stability will flow from that" (cited in Khader 2013, 24). The introduction of the ENP was a response to the new security situation developed in the EU's near abroad and a policy designed to also support EU efforts to realize the objectives of the European Security Strategy (ESS) that was adopted in December of 2003. The ESS was rather explicit in defining the neighborhood "as a key geographical priority of EU external action" (EC 2003b, 9).

The ENP was based on a Communication entitled "Wider Europe – Neighbourhood" adopted by the European Commission (EC) in 2003 and whose main objective was the strengthening of the stability and security of the EU and its neighboring states (EC 2003a). The ENP is meant to allow EU Members States to work "together with partner countries, to define a set of priorities, whose fulfillment will bring them closer to the European Union" (EC 2004, 1). Even though candidacy for EU membership was not foreseen, the EU nevertheless emphasized the importance for building communication and shared values related to issues such as security, democracy, human rights, political freedom, and trade liberalization. According to the ESS, "stability for not just the member states, but also the surrounding regions could be ensured much more effectively with attention paid to these areas, which are clearly interrelated and hard to untangle from one another" (EC 2003b, 3). To achieve its goals, the ENP sought to utilize a range of conditionality-related instruments the use of which was to be guided by the ESS objectives.

Since its launch in 2004, the ENP has evolved considerably, due to a number of radical changes and challenges affecting the neighboring countries in terms of stability, prosperity and security.

The European Neighborhood Policy (ENP)

According to the EES (2003b, 4) threats to the EU may emerge as the result of regional conflicts which could lead to extremism, terrorism, state failure, organized crime, weapons of mass destruction (WMD) proliferation and refugee and immigration flows. Violent or frozen conflicts and problems such as those in the Middle East were thus viewed as having the potential of impacting European interests and security directly and indirectly. Particularly, bad governance – reflected in corruption, abuse of power, weak or collapsed institutions and lack of accountability – was regarded as a key threat to EU security (ESS 2003b, 4). Therefore, spreading good governance, supporting social and political reform, dealing with corruption and abuse of power, establishing the rule of law and protecting human rights were viewed by the EU as the best means for increasing European security.

The main ENP objective was to strengthen stability, security and wellbeing in the Union's near abroad as a means to strengthen European security. The policy was designed to prevent the emergence of new dividing lines between the enlarged EU and its neighbors and to offer them the chance to participate in various EU activities, through greater political, security, economic and cultural cooperation (EC 2004, 3).

The method proposed to achieve the ENP objective was that the EU would work together with its MENA partners to define a set of priorities whose fulfillment would bring them closer to the European Union. These priorities were incorporated in jointly agreed Action Plans, which set out an agenda of political and economic reforms with short and medium-term priorities of three to five years covering a number of key areas for specific action, such as political dialogue and reform; trade and measures preparing partners for gradually obtaining a stake in the EU's internal market; justice and home affairs; energy, transport, information society, environment and research and innovation; and social policy and people-to-people contacts (EC 2004, 3).

The EU's relationship with its MENA neighbors was to be built on mutual commitment to common values principally within the fields of the rule of law, good governance, the respect for human and minority rights, the promotion of good neighborly relations, and the principles of market economy and sustainable development. Moreover, the level of ambition of the EU's relationships with its neighbors was to take into account the extent to which these values are effectively shared (EC 2004, 3). The EU also expected its MENA partners to abide by international law and collaborate in conflict resolution, the fight against terrorism and WMD proliferation.

The ENP is mainly a bilateral policy built upon legal agreements, such as the Partnership and Cooperation Agreements (PCA) or Association Agreements (AA) which determine the relations between the EU and each individual MENA country. However, the ENP was designed to reinforce existing forms of regional and sub-regional cooperation and provide a framework for their further development. To this end, the ENP document contained recommendations on the development of regional cooperation and integration, as a means to address certain issues arising at the enlarged EU's external borders. Thus, the ENP was complemented by regional multilateral co-operation initiatives, such as the EMP and the Union for the Mediterranean (UfM).

Specifically, in regard to the MENA region, the ENP sought to further regional integration by building on the EMP achievements, notably in the area of trade, and invited the MENA countries to promote infrastructure interconnections and networks, as well as develop new forms of cooperation with their neighbors (EC 2004, 4). The ENP also sought to reinforce efforts to meet the objectives of the ESS in the Mediterranean and the Middle East (EC 2004, 6).

The basic principles of the ENP were: "joint ownership" and "differentiation". "Joint ownership" of the process was to be based on the awareness of shared values and common interests between the EU and its MENA partners. The ENP document explicitly stated that the EU did not "seek to impose priorities or conditions on its partners" and that there was "no question of asking partners to accept a pre-determined set of priorities" (EC 2004, 8). Thus, the proposed Action Plans were to be defined by common consent and they would vary from country to country, while their success was dependent on the clear recognition of mutual interests in addressing a set of priority issues. The ambition and the pace of development of the EU's relationship with each partner country was dependent on its degree of commitment to common values, as well as its will and capacity to implement agreed priorities (EC 2004, 8).

As far as the principle of "differentiation" is concerned, the ENP document specified that the drawing up of the Action Plans and the priorities agreed with each partner would depend on its particular circumstances and they could differ with respect to geographic location, the political and economic situation, relations with the EU and with neighboring countries, reform programs, needs and capacities, commitment to shared values, as well as perceived interests in the context of the ENP (EC 2004, 8).

In the ENP framework, the EU sought to use financial and diplomatic means to ensure that there was a move towards democratization and market liberalization in its MENA neighbors. In other words, the EU intended to use a strategy of positive reinforcement where the reward for desired behavior was financial assistance.

Implementation of the ENP is jointly promoted and monitored through the Committees and sub-Committees established in the frame of the PCA or AA agreements. The European Commission and the High Representative of the European Union for Foreign Affairs and Security Policy would publish Annual Reports assessing the progress made towards the objectives of the Action Plans and the Association Agendas.

To assist with political and economic reforms, the EU committed to providing financial support in grant form to its MENA partners, while the European Investment Bank and the European Bank for Reconstruction and Development complement the EU's support through loans. MENA countries have also been eligible for support under a number of other EU instruments, such as the Instrument Contributing to Peace and Stability, Humanitarian Aid, and the European Instrument for Democracy and Human Rights. Yet, MENA countries have been eligible to participate in EU internal programs, such as those of research and innovation, energy, transport, culture, education and youth (Erasmus+). Participation of MENA partners in EU programs and agencies is meant to promote reform and modernization in the MENA neighborhood and strengthen administrative and regulatory convergence of MENA countries with the EU.

In 2007, the European Council authorized the participation of MENA countries in activities of a large number of EU agencies, such as FRONTEX, EUROPOL, CEPOL, EEA, EFSA, and EMCDDA. The relevant Agencies' Regulations provide for various options of participation, allowing for different levels of engagement and working arrangements. All MENA countries have some form of cooperation with those EU agencies.

Despite its various commitments, the EU's approach to the MENA region suffered from some major weaknesses. Although human rights, democracy promotion, and conflict resolution were central to the ENP, there was a significant discrepancy between EU rhetoric and practice. Specifically, the

EU's involvement in the Arab–Israeli conflict resolution was mainly declaratory and often hesitant and incoherent (Khader 2013, 9). For example, while reiterating its condemnation of Israeli policies in the Occupied Territories, the EU sought to reinforce its ties with Israel placing at the same time the Palestinians/Arabs and Israelis on the same footing. Moreover, questions of human rights and democracy did not take priority as the EU settled for a more realist approach to MENA politics while the Arab civil society was not been taken seriously in the EU–MENA dialogue. By sidelining civil society actors and with the gradual prioritization of security over reform, the EU contributed indirectly to the political *status quo* and undermined the application of the principle of "differentiation". However, one of the more important reasons for the ENP contestation was the EU's tendency to disregard advice and instead provide 'lessons' thereby jeopardizing the application of the "joint ownership" principle. In other words, the EU did not cultivate an image of a "credible partner", learning to "listen to unfamiliar voices" and speaking to important actors of Arab civil society. This led the Arab world to think that the EU was simply interested in exporting its institutional model and value system.

As some had already predicted (Bosse 2007; Sasse 2008), the ENP's 'top-down', 'one size fits all' approach failed to produce the expected results. Then the outbreak of the Arab Spring in 2010 not only took the EU by surprise and added to the contestation of the EU norms, values and practices but also dispelled many myths circulating in Europe, such as that the Arabs were not interested in, concerned by or prepared for democracy; that pro-Western dictators are better bets than the Islamist alternative; that the Arab World was a fiction and that the cross-border appeal of Arab identity had waned; and that authoritarian regimes are unshakable (Khader 2013, 33–34). Instead the Arab Spring demonstrated that the Arab public opinion is diversified and rational, that there have always been forces for change in the MENA region and that there is a vibrant civil society in spite of all forms of coercive state control.

The strong contestation of ENP conditionality by MENA countries in conjunction with the Arab Spring-related events forced the EU to respond urgently to the new challenges.

The 2011 ENP Review

The EU's response was first enshrined in the "Partnership for Democracy and Shared Prosperity" of March 2011 (EC 2011a). This document noted that the EU needed "to support the wish of the people in our neighbourhood" through a "qualitative step forward" in "a joint commitment" to "common values: democracy, human rights, social justice, good governance and the rule of the law" (EC 2011a, 2). The new approach was to be based on greater "differentiation", conditionality and "mutual accountability" and built on three elements: democratic transformation and institution building, stronger partnership with the people, and sustainable and inclusive growth (EC 2011a, 3). To support its new initiative, the EU established on 21 September 2011 a new aid package entitled "Strengthening Partnership and Inclusive Growth" (SPRING).

"Differentiation" was to be determined according to the application of the "more for more" principle, which introduced a new incentive-based approach (EC 2011a, 5). The purpose of the "more for more" principle is to reward faster reform by greater support in terms of aid, trade and advanced relationship status with the Union. The assessments contained in the Annual Progress Reports of the European Commission (EC) and the European External Action Service (EEAS) form the basis for EU policy towards each MENA partner under the 'more for more' principle. MENA countries advancing political reforms are offered additional elements of market access and a greater share of the EU financial support. In this context, the SPRING program was intended for those MENA partners that undertake clear and concrete steps towards political reform.

However, in the eyes of the MENA partners, the "more and more principle" is similar to the previous rhetoric of tailor-made approaches. It continued to over-rely on neoliberal capitalist market economy recipes based on an "almost sacred belief in liberalisation and privatisation" (Soler and Viilup 2011, 4). Moreover, according to the "more for more" principle, any MENA country which engages in "deep and sustainable democracy" will be rewarded with "upgraded status", increased aid and enhanced political dialogue. However, it is questionable whether MENA countries were ready or willing to accept and fully implement external prescriptions, even in exchange for reward. Yet, the 2011 ENP Review did not clarify who sets the benchmarks of "deep reform" or who is entitled to make the performance assessment or to what degree MENA countries would be involved in the assessment process. Likewise, the meaning of "mutual accountability" is unclear as the ENP Review did not clarify whether MENA countries could hold the EU accountable for its shortcomings or how "mutual accountability" should be exercised and enforced.

The principles of "more and more" and "mutual accountability" were not discussed with all the relevant MENA stakeholders. How could a new approach to old problems be adopted without being open to the input of those concerned? This is a fundamental question which explains, to a large extent, the negative reaction of Arab social networks to the revised ENP which was characterized as a "non-consensus response". Thus, the employment of the "more and more" and "mutual accountability" principles invited the question of local ownership and undermined the principles of "joint ownership" and "differentiation". Moreover, the absence of input by the MENA partners could make it easy for the EU to shift its policy from "carrots to sticks" (Oxfam, 2011, 5).

The EU's response to the new challenges also found its expression in the EC Communication entitled "A New Response to a Changing Neighbourhood", which was published in May 2011 (EC 2011b). In this Communication, the EU reasserted that "partnership with our neighbours is mutually beneficial," but must be based on "mutual accountability", a shared commitment to universal values, a higher degree of differentiation, comprehensive institution-building, and imperative and deep democracy (EC 2011b, 2). The Communication added that "the EU does not seek to impose a model or a ready-made recipe for political reform" (EC 2011b, 2).

The 2011 Review put a strong focus on the promotion of 'deep and sustainable' democracy, accompanied by inclusive economic development. 'Deep and sustainable' democracy was to include free and fair elections, freedom of expression, of assembly and of association, judicial independence, fight against corruption and democratic control over the armed forces (EC 2011b, 3). To achieve 'deep and sustainable' democracy, the EU proposed the establishment of a European Endowment for Democracy and a Civil Society Facility (CSF).

Through the Civil Society Facility instrument, the EU aims to "support civil society organisations, to develop their advocacy capacity, their ability to monitor reform and their implementing and evaluating EU programmes" (EC 2011b, 4). This support was deemed essential since it would enable civil society organizations to voice concerns, contribute to policy making, hold governments accountable, and ensure that economic growth is geared towards poverty alleviation and inclusive growth.

The Civil Society Facility proposal, however, was met with skepticism by Arab civil society organizations – as in the recent past, EU-allocated financial support was insufficient, bureaucratic hurdles discouraging and disbursement very slow. Moreover, the selection of civil society organizations to be funded has often been inadequate and sometimes arbitrary as the EU engaged more with civil society organizations perceived more agreeable and acceptable than others with a real social base (Khader 2011, 37). Thus, the EU was criticized for taking the driving seat thereby delegitimizing a transition led by the people and for not being interested in more transparency in the relations between external donors and local actors.

The European Endowment for Democracy instrument seeks to promote the creation of civil society organizations and provide assistance to trade unions and other social actors, such as non-registered non-governmental organizations (EC 2011b, 4). Apart from supporting local actors, including political movements, journalists and NGOs, the EED provided a forum where MENA states were to share their experiences with the Central and Eastern European Countries (CEECs) which went through a significant political, social, and economic transformation on their way to becoming EU members. The CEECs had important comparative advantages because, unlike some of the EU Members States, they were not colonial powers (Giusti and Fassi 2014, 119).

The May 2001 Communication also called for the creation of a "Deep and Comprehensive Free Trade Area" (DCFTA) (EC 2011b, 9). The implementation of the DCFTA gives MENA neighbors a possibility to integrate into the EU internal market without becoming an EU member state. Modelled after the EU's agreements with pre-accession states, DCFTAs are very extensive in the commitments by EU neighbors to approximate to a significant amount of EU *acquis communautaire*. In other words, the DCFTAs go beyond strictly trade-related matters and imply serious domestic change to achieve the necessary convergence.

The idea of a "Deep and Comprehensive Free Trade Area" also raised considerable skepticism, as in authoritarian states liberalization and privatization often lead to the concentration of economic power in the hands of a minority, impeding growth to trickle down to the vast majority of the population. In fact, this has been the experience in the MENA countries since the imposition of the structural adjustment programs by the International Monetary Fund where hastily imposed privatization transformed plan economies into clan economies (Khader 2011, 38). Therefore, many actors in MENA countries considered it unwise for the EU to attach economic policy conditions such as liberalization and that "support for economic growth should be rooted in support for peoples' choices of a revised economic model" (Oxfam 2011, 3).

Yet, MENA countries, which are in democratic transition are facing significant economic challenges. Thus, their first priority is to put their economies in order and address urgent questions of poverty and development. Consequently, a "Deep and Comprehensive Free Trade Area" is not an immediate goal. This is the reason for which it has been suggested that the EU should show flexibility by adapting its approach to changing circumstances and that its emphasis should be placed on poverty alleviation, women's empowerment, gender equality, youth participation, job creation and sustainable development. Another suggestion is that the EU should promote regional integration as a way to increase trade volume. Furthermore, for MENA countries, the search for more equitable economic relations is more urgent than mere liberalization policies. In this respect, assistance programs are expected to be put in place to bolster competitiveness, innovation and knowledge technology.

In their meeting of 3 December 2013, the EEAS and the EC Directorate General for Development and Cooperation outlined the conditions for the participation of MENA countries to various EU programs while in early 2014 the EU decided that assistance to MENA countries was now to be provided mainly through the European Neighbourhood Instrument (ENI), which was established as a successor to the European Neighbourhood and Partnership Instrument (ENPI). The ENI was designed to further strengthen certain key features of the former ENPI, notably greater differentiation between countries based on progress with reforms. For the ENI purposes, the EU allocated a total budget of €15.4 billion for the period from 2014 to 2020; a very high amount that represents 24% of expenditures for the EU's external action. The ENI funds are channeled through bilateral programs, as well as multi-country and cross-border cooperation programs.

The Shortcomings of the 2011 Review

Despite the 2011 Review, the diffusion of EU norms and values in the MENA region has been ineffective because these norms and values are locally contested by societies experiencing transition from authoritarian to democratic regimes (Tholens and Groß 2015). Manasi Singh (2016, 32) believes that it is the "…unintended consequences of the EU's misconceived and ill-informed policies that have made its neighborhood more politically fragmented and unstable" and that by

> …holding up democracy as an unquestionable value and as end in itself, the EU takes for granted that democracy and political reform is external to the region, and thus can be successfully exported.

The diffusion of EU norms and values in the MENA region became a matter of contestation for three broad reasons: first, because of their ambiguous nature; second, due to the potential conflicts between them (in particular between political and economic values) resulting in policy incoherence; and third, due to the existence of competing values in the Arab world (Gstöhl 2015; Del Sarto 2016).

Specifically, there are three ambiguities in regard to the EU's values. First, these values are, in theory, already shared and form the basis for developing relations with MENA countries (Cremona 2011, 301). First, Article 21(1) of the TEU requires the Union to seek to build partnerships with countries that "share the principles on which it is founded." This implies that unless countries share the values and principles on which the EU is founded, they cannot enter into a partnership with the Union. But since the MENA countries have joined the ENP, this means that they already share these EU values and principles. As a result, there is no reason to respond to further EU requests for 'value sharing'.

Second, the EU uses the notion of 'common values' both as a universal and an EU concept (Leino and Petrov 2009, 656). Consequently, views between the EU and the MENA countries have differed in reference to what kind of democracy or market economy should be promoted. A third ambiguity concerns how the values should be implemented (Kochenov 2014, 53). For example, while conditionality may promote the transmission of EU *acquis*, the latter may be not a suitable instrument for the export of those values which MENA countries needed to internalize (Gstöhl 2015, 4).

The substance and coherence of the EU have also been questioned (Gstöhl 2015, 4). To begin with, the pursuit of economic interests and of democratization or political stability may enter into conflict. For example, despite that in the official EU documents political, social and economic rights received equal treatment, in practice more attention has been focused on political rather than economic values. As Stefania Panebianco (2006, 141) has argued, in EU practice "economic liberalization and the establishment of free markets – which are also crucial EU values – seem to come before human rights and democratic principles." Hence, the EU encountered the challenge of how to prioritize among competing ENP goals such as security, good governance and economic aspirations for if not, it risks damaging its credibility.

Moreover, conflicts may also arise within the same group of values, such as between poverty reduction and trade liberalization or between political stability and democratization (Börzel and van Hüllen 2014). For example, EU has been very skeptical about Islamist parties winning free elections in MENA countries, while during the Arab Spring, the Union prioritized its security concerns at the expense of the establishment of democracy in the region. Yet, in contrast to what happens in the EU, many of the MENA countries are governed by authoritarian regimes, while political Islam has been on the rise in Turkey and the Arab world where Muslim societies appear to favor a role for religious leaders in politics.

According to Sienglinde Gstöhl (2015, 8–12), the mechanisms of value export have been challenged for three reasons: first, because some MENA countries have been incapable and/or unwilling to absorb the EU norms and values; second, the EU and its member states have failed to conduct a consistent and credible policy; and third, the EU is facing normative rivalry from other actors. In other words, ENP faces challenges of capacity, consistency and competition (Gstöhl 2016).

Specifically, a precondition for a successful value and norm transference is the political will in the MENA countries to tackle the domestic reforms required. But in authoritarian regimes, the export of EU norms and values depends on the political costs involved in adopting reforms. In other words, the EU's challenge is how to convince authoritarian governments to implement democratic reforms when these governments view such EU norms and values as threatening their own hold on power (Pace 2007, 663). Moreover, the resonance of EU values is not the same in all societies. For instance, it has been argued that transition countries tend to be more receptive to EU norms than authoritarian regimes because they are likely to be more open to new ideas after their old governance systems were discredited (Checkel 2005, 813). Second, a lack of absorption capacity negatively impacts political and economic reforms. For economies lacking strong institutions and administrative capacities, the implementation of EU standards can involve high costs. Consequently, it can be questioned whether certain EU instruments are the most suitable instruments for countries facing serious development challenges (Leino and Petrov 2009, 665). Yet, a country's commitment to adopt and implement EU norms does not necessarily mean that this is actually followed up by their transposition into domestic law, nor by their application (Langbein and Wolczuk 2012). The transmission of EU values is also affected by inadequacies on the side of the European Union. First, due to the unwillingness of the EU institutions or its member states to deliver certain incentives, such as the prospect of obtaining EU membership, the EU's ability to deliver real incentives to MENA countries remains constrained.

Second, the non-participation of MENA countries in the decision-making process about the actual meaning of common values further adds to the constraints facing the EU while at the same time preventing the internalization of norms in the MENA region (Leino and Petrov 2009, 666). As non-EU actual or prospective members, the MENA countries face some risks while becoming involved with the European Union. For instance, the conclusion of agreements between the EU and the MENA countries involves the adoption of and adaptation to the EU *acquis*, its uniform interpretation as well as an independent monitoring and judicial enforcement. Without participation in the relevant EU decision making processes, such a "degree of supranationality encroaches upon national autonomy" (Gstöhl 2015, 10).

Third, the lack of capacity and/or willingness to offer the MENA countries certain benefits or to endorse the values by responding to non-compliance may generate inconsistent EU policies. For example, as it was noted previously, the EU's promotion of human rights and democracy in the neighborhood has frequently been trumped by economic or security interests. At the same time, the EU's engagement with autocratic regimes in MENA countries is potentially dangerous as it undermines the Union's strategic goal to democratize its immediate neighborhood (Kurki 2013, 230). In addition, in contrast to the EU institutions, the EU member states often ignore conditionality in their bilateral dealings with MENA countries. But, for the EU's policies to be effective, EU member states must be willing to support EU conditionality instead of undermining it.

Finally, the role of external competitors may play a role because of competing mechanisms of value export. The EU's efforts of value promotion assume that the European model of democracy and market economy can and should be exported. However, this assumption may be questioned not only by the MENA countries themselves but also by external actors. For example, in the MENA region, several countries, such as Tunisia, Egypt, Libya and Syria, rebelled against Western backed authoritarian rulers, while some countries also experienced powerful counter-revolutions. The regimes in the Gulf States tried to 'buy off' their citizens and supported regressive forces in the region, while Morocco and Jordan implemented rather cosmetic domestic reforms (Leonard 2014). Democracy promotion implies that the EU must engage in dialogue with all political groups and not just those that mirror Western values. Political Islam is not a unitary force but characterized by important splits between different interpretations of Islam. As it has been argued, the political awakening in the Arab Spring "is about people claiming democratic rights to emancipate themselves from the traditional influence of the West, rather than trying to join it" (Leonard 2014).

Therefore, despite its 2011 Review the ENP failed to recognize and address the nature of economic and political challenges facing the MENA region as a whole. As a result, in 2015, the EU launched a new effort to revive the ENP with the European Commission calling for "a need to understand better the different aspirations, values, and interests of our partners" (EC 2015, 1).

The 2015 Review

The launch of the 2015 Review took place in parallel with the work conducted on the EU's Global Strategy, which also aims for the stabilization of the EU's Neighborhood through building up the resilience of its partners.

As in the previous EC Communications, good governance, democracy, the rule of law and human rights; economic development for stabilization; security; and migration and mobility remain the core ENP areas, while the 2015 EC Communication listed the differentiation amongst partner countries, flexibility, joint ownership, greater involvement of the EU Member States, and shared responsibility are identified as the key principles of the 2015 Review (EC 2015).

The differentiated partnerships and the tailor-made approach remained the hallmarks of the 2015 Review. For MENA countries who have agreed with the EU Partnership Priorities, Association Agendas, Action Plans or other similar jointly agreed documents, the 2015 Review foresees the adoption of a multiannual programming document in the form of a single support framework. For the remaining MENA countries, multiannual programming documents take the form of the strategy papers & multiannual indicative programs. This approach applies also to multi-country and cross-border cooperation programs (EC 2015, 4).

As far as the effectiveness of the implementation of the "more and more" principle is concerned, the EC recognized that too few MENA countries introduced political reforms and noted that "the EU should explore more effective ways to take its case for fundamental reforms with partners, including through engagement with civil, economic and social actors" (EC 2015, 5).

To apply the "differentiation" principle, country-by-country developments are addressed in factual country-specific reports which are released by the EEAS and the EC ahead of the Association Council meetings or other similar high-level events and replace the previous ENP Annual Reports, which used to be released for all partners at the same time (EC 2015, 4). The Association Councils remain the highest formal bodies established to supervise the implementation of the Agreements and to discuss issues of mutual interest. However, the 2015 Review did not clarify if the preparation of these documents is to take account of the views of the MENA partners. This has been a strong point of contestation for MENA countries since unilateral EU assessment has been seen as undermining the "joint ownership" principle.

The 2015 Review reinforced the principle of flexibility in order to accelerate assistance and to ensure it is better adapted to rapidly evolving political circumstances and priorities (EC 2015, 19–20). Apart from providing ENI grants, the EU has also sought to leverage substantial additional funding through cooperation with International Financial Institutions and by means of investment subsidies from the Neighbourhood Investment Facility. Technical assistance instruments are also available to MENA countries to help implement Association Agendas and Partnership Priorities.

As previously, the EU objectives and priorities for partner countries together with indicative allocations are set in relevant multiannual programming documents, which are, in principle, established in partnership with the beneficiary MENA countries. In this respect, the objectives and priorities of EU support are to be developed in consultation with the relevant authorities of the MENA partners, as well as civil society organizations and other stakeholders. Yet, with the 2015 Review, the EU objectives and priorities are to be set in coordination with Member States and other donors, including International Financial Institutions, while the programming is also subject of a Strategic Dialogue with the European Parliament.

The 2015 Review acknowledges that cooperation between the EU and its MENA partners on migration-related issues should be strengthened to facilitate mobility and at the same time discourage irregular migration. The goal is to develop, under the auspices of the European Agenda for Migration, mobility partnerships and other agreements ensuring that the movement of persons between the EU and its MENA partners is well managed (EC 2015, 16–17). Moreover, the 2015 Review has opened up a wide range of new areas of cooperation between the EU and MENA countries, including conflict prevention, crisis management and security sector reform. The new approach covers all security areas in a combination of bilateral, regional, and cross-border projects. Through its new approach, the EU seeks to intensify work with MENA countries to tackle terrorism and to counter radicalization. To this end, the EU views the role of the civil society as central in the identification of partnership priorities (EC 2015, 12–14). Furthermore, as part of its regional focus, the EU has sought to strengthen its operational cooperation with the League of Arab States through common participation to Working Groups dealing with conflict prevention, early warning and crisis management, humanitarian assistance, counter-terrorism, transnational organized crime, and WMD proliferation and arms control.

Conclusion

To investigate whether the 2015 Review ensures a "differentiated" approach to partners, "joint ownership", and more flexibility in the use of EU instruments, the EC published a "Report on the Implementation of the European Neighbourhood Policy" in May 2017 (EC 2017). This Report, however, has mainly provided an overview of the EU activities since the 2015 Review was adopted rather than a complete and comprehensive assessment of its effectiveness. Therefore, it remains to be seen whether in the spirit of the "joint ownership", "mutual accountability" and "mutual responsibility" principles the EU would be open to questions, criticism and suggestions from its MENA partners and whether MENA countries would play any role in setting the benchmarks of deep reform, have a say in how relevant EU policies develop and apply or would be involved in the performance assessment.

A more effective engagement with the MENA region would require the EU to abolish neocolonial attitudes reflecting a 'civilizer–civilizee' relationship. Instead, the EU could become more open to the perceptions and viewpoints of its MENA neighbors and cultivate a relationship of mutual respect and equal partnership.

References

Börzel, Tanja and Vera Van Hüllen. 2014. "One voice, One Message, but Conflicting Goals: Cohesiveness and Consistency in the European Neighborhood Policy." *Journal of European Public Policy*, 21(7): 1033–1049.

Bosse, Giselle. 2007. "Values in the EU's Neighborhood Policy: Political Rhetoric or Reflection of a coherent policy?" *European Political Economy Review* 7: 38–62.

Checkel, Jeffrey, T. 2005. "International Institutions and Socialization in Europe: Introduction and Framework." *International Organization, 59*(4), 801–826.

Cremona, Marise. 2011. "Values in EU Foreign Policy." In *Beyond the Established Orders: Policy Interconnections between the EU and the Rest of the World*, edited by Malcolm Evans and Panos Koutrakos. Oxford: Hurst Publishers.

Del Sarto, Raffaella A. 2016. "Normative Empire Europe: The European Union, Its Borderlands, and the 'Arab Spring.'"*Journal of Common Market Studies,* 54(2): 215–232.

European Commission. 2003a. *Wider Europe – Neighbourhood: A New Framework for Relations with Our Eastern and Southern Neighbours*, 11 March 2003, COM (2003) 104 final. http://eeas.europa.eu/archives/docs/enp/pdf/pdf/com03_104_en.pdf

European Commission. 2003b. *European Security Strategy: A Secure Europe in a Better World.* http://www.consilium.europa.eu/uedocs/cmsUpload/78367.pdf

European Commission. 2004. *European Neighbourhood Policy*, 12 May 2004, COM(2004) 373 final. https://ec.europa.eu/neighbourhood-enlargement/sites/near/files/2004_communication_from_the_commission_-_european_neighbourhood_policy_-_strategy_paper.pdf

European Commission. 2011a. *A Partnership for Democracy and Shared Prosperity with the Southern Mediterranean*. https://ec.europa.eu/research/iscp/pdf/policy/com_2011_200_en.pdf

European Commission. 2011b. *A New Response to a Changing Neighbourhood: A Review of the European Neighbourhood Policy*. https://www.ab.gov.tr/files/ardb/evt/1_avrupa_birligi/1_9_komsuluk_politikalari/A_review_of_European_Neighbourhood_Policy.pdf

European Commission. 2015. *Towards a New European Neighbourhood Policy*. https://ec.europa.eu/neighbourhood-enlargement/sites/near/files/neighbourhood/consultation/consultation.pdf

European Commission. 2017. *Report on the Implementation of the European Neighbourhood Policy Review*. Brussels, 18 May 2017. https://eeas.europa.eu/sites/eeas/files/2_en_act_part1_v9_3.pdf

Gstöhl, Sieglinde. 2016. "The Contestation of Values in the European Neighbourhood Policy: Challenges of Capacity, Consistency and Competition." In *The European Neighbourhood Policy – Values and Principles*, edited by S. Poli. Abingdon: Routledge, 58–78.

Gstöhl, Sieglinde. 2015. "The Contestation of values in the European Neighborhood Policy: Challenges of Capacity, Consistency and Competition." Paper presented at the EUSA Fourteenth Biennial Conference. Boston, 5–7 March.

Khader, B. (2013). *The European Union and the Arab World*. Barcelona: IEMed.

Kochenov, Dimitry. 2014. "The Issue of Values." In *Legislative Approximation and Application of EU Law in the Eastern Neighbourhood of the European Union: Towards a Common Regulatory Space?* edited by Peter Van Elsuwege and Roman Petrov. London: Routledge.

Kurki, M. 2013. *Democratic Futures: Revisioning Democracy Promotion and Democratization*. London: Routledge.

Langbein, Julia & Kataryna Wolczuk. 2011. "Convergence without membership? The impact of the European Union in the neighbourhood." *Journal of European Public Policy*, 19:6, 863–881.

Leino, Parvi and Roman Petrov. 2009. "Beyond 'Common Values' and competing Universals – the Promotion of the EU's Common Values through the European Neighborhood Policy." *European Law Journal* 15(5): 654–671.

Leonard, Mark. 2014. "Seven reasons why the Arab uprisings are eclipsing Western values." European Council of Foreign Relations, 23 January.

Oxfam. 2011. *Power to the People? Reactions to the EU's response to the Arab Spring*. Oxfam Briefing Note, 14 November 2011.

Pace, Michael. 2007. "Norm Shifting from EMP to ENP: The EU as a Norm Entrepreneur in the South? *Cambridge Review of International Affairs* 20(4): 659–675.

Panebianco, Stefania. 2006. The constraints in the EU actions as a "norm exporter" in the Mediterranean. In Elgstrom and Smith (eds.), *The European Union's Roles in International Politics*, 136–154.

Sasse, Gwendolyn. 2008. "The European Neighbourhood Policy: Conditionality Revisited for the EU's Eastern Neighbours." *Europe-Asia Studies* 60(2): 295–316.

Soler E. and E. Viilup. 2011. "Reviewing the Neighbourhood Policy: A weak response to fast changing realities." *Notes internacionals*. Barcelona, CIDOB, No. 36, June 2011.

Singh, Manasi. 2016. "The EU's Democracy Promotion in Its 'Neighborhood': Renegotiating the Post-Arab Spring Framework." In *Democracy and Civil Society in a Global Era*, edited by Scott Nicholas Romaniuk and Marguerite Marlin. London: Routledge, 31–42.

Tholens, Simone and Lisa Groß. 2015. "Diffusion, contestation and localization in post-war states: 20 years of Western Balkans reconstruction." *Journal of International Relations & Development,* 18: 249–264.

8

The United Nations and Middle Eastern Security

ALLISON MILLER

The United Nations (UN) serves many important purposes within the context of global governance. Thomas Weiss (2016) argues that as peoples and states become more interconnected, there is a need for more effective international management. He points to global issues such as terrorism, refugee movements, climate change, and economic crises as evidence for the need of international management. The Middle East is facing issues that encompass the entire aforementioned list, plus many others. The United Nations is subject to constant criticism from actors within the international community, be it from individual citizens, all forms of media platforms, or official governing bodies. Though sometimes UN criticism is valid and necessary, it is important to remember the contributions the UN has made in the Middle East. It is a fact that there is more that the UN could do to work towards regional stability and security in the Middle East. It is also a fact that the UN is operating under strained resources in highly complex issues that often involve power struggles among various external nations, which have geopolitical interests in the region.

The UN is not a perfect system representing a global governing body. As an institution, the UN does what it can with what it has. This should never be forgotten nor taken for granted. Whether it is by supplying peacekeepers or providing developmental or humanitarian aid, the UN works to protect the lives of millions of people across the Middle East. Occasionally, this is in the form of peacekeepers, but it can also be in the form of providing critically needed medical equipment, providing training for local residents in conflict zones to increase resilience, or providing education for children whose lives have been uprooted by conflict. The fact of the matter is that it is better to have the UN in whatever capacity that is possible than to not have it at all.

The purpose of this chapter is to explore the UN's contributions to peace and stability in the Middle East in the post-Cold War era. Utilizing the Middle East as a broad case study allows for a conceptual framework for how the UN operationalizes security. Moreover, the Middle East case helps us comprehend how the regional affects the global, as well as why interdependence matters. The traditional approach of peacekeeping in the Middle East has now evolved into an approach that also seeks to work towards regional security by emphasizing human security. This reframing has resulted in the UN supplying developmental and humanitarian aid in various ways. Though there are many examples in the Middle East that would support this development, this chapter focuses on Lebanon, Gaza and Israel, Iraq and ISIS, the Syrian civil war, and Yemen. Each section addresses the security concerns that currently exist and highlights what the UN is doing to alleviate them.

Lebanon

The United Nations Interim Force in Lebanon (UNIFIL) has been present since its creation by the UN Security Council in March 1978 (UNIFIL Fact Sheet n.d.). Headquartered in Naqoura, southern Lebanon, the mission includes monitoring the cessation of hostilities, providing support to the Lebanese military, and providing humanitarian assistance to civilian populations (UNIFIL Fact Sheet n.d.). In April 2000, the Secretary-General received official notice from the Government of Israel that outlined their plan to withdraw Israeli forces from Southern Lebanon (UNIFIL Background n.d.). Since then, a large role of the UNIFIL has been to monitor the border between Israel and Lebanon and report any violations perpetrated by either the Israeli Defense Forces (IDF) or the Lebanese military. The area monitored by UNIFIL is most commonly known as the *Blue Line*, which is a 120 kilometer stretch from Ras al-Naqoura in south-western Lebanon to Shab'a in south-eastern Lebanon (Pokharel 2016).

The Lebanese Armed Forces (LAF) and UNIFIL coordinate with one another in order to ensure the security of the Blue Line – which faces numerous security concerns. The LAF and UNIFIL conduct joint military and training exercises, exchange experiences through a joint lecture program, and conduct checkpoints and patrols together (UNIFIL Operations n.d.). It is through these types of coordinated efforts that the UN has successfully implemented a long-term protective dimension in regard to security. UNIFIL regularly mediates tripartite meetings between senior officials of the LAF and IDF that serve as an essential method for addressing conflict management and building bridges and confidence between the parties (Tripartite 2017). UNIFIL has been largely successful at creating a positive relationship with the LAF that increases the physical security of the Blue Line and holds both sides accountable for any violations of mandates.

Aside from engaging with the LAF, UNIFIL also recognizes the importance of engaging with the local populations. UNIFIL does this by informing local civilians of UNIFIL mandates and activities, providing assistance when possible, engaging with local culture, customs, and concerns, as well as actively participating in community events. Civilian Affairs and Civil Military Coordination serve as the main interface through which UNIFIL and local communities interact. Through these interfaces, UNIFIL is able to engage with government and community leaders, key religious figures, civil society groups, and international organizations that are involved with development initiatives. Creating a cohesive environment between UNIFIL and the local communities in which they carry out operations is a key aspect in maintaining security along the Blue Line. Understanding and engaging with local culture and activities provides a unique platform for UNIFIL to do this successfully. UNIFIL also provides free basic services to local populations, such as medical, dental, and veterinarian services. This helps to form a level of trust that is necessary for ensuring the security of the local populations as they deal with the day-to-day concerns that arise from being located in an area where personal security is a concern.

The UN is also involved with the refugee population in Lebanon. Lebanon houses a large population of Syrian refugees that result from the ongoing war in Syria. The United Nations High Commissioner for Refugees (UNHCR) is tasked for addressing the needs of the refugee population in Lebanon, which is numbered around 1.5 million. The Syrian refugee population in Lebanon should be considered as highly vulnerable as large numbers deal with concerns over legal residency, which makes it difficult to work, send children to school, or receive health care. The concern over residency also prevents birth registration which puts tens of thousands of Syrian children born in Lebanon at risk of statelessness. This amounts to an increasing security concern both in the sense that vulnerable populations are not having basic needs met as well as vulnerable children not obtaining citizenship to any country. The residency issues Syrian refugees face creates a culture of fear and raises concerns of exploitation – such as labor exploitation and sexual abuse – as refugees with expired or no residency fear arrest by police (Human Rights Watch 2017).

The UNHCR plays an active role in attempting to address the needs of Syrian refugees in Lebanon, but they are not able to address these with the necessary capacity. For example, in 2017 only 170,000 Syrian refugees received winterization support from the UNHCR (UNHCR n.d.). Refugees must endure harsh weather during the winter and become susceptible of freezing to death if basic needs are not met. The international community should take a more active role in providing funding for such basic needs to the UNHCR. Properly addressing basic human needs is a critical element to security as the population at hand is already vulnerable and susceptible to experiencing human rights abuses.

Gaza and Israel

Gaza represents a high security concern in the Middle East in terms of living conditions, economic stability, and protective security. It is an area that has experienced a high level of violence due to decades old conflict over territorial disputes. Hamas maintains control over Gaza – and the citizens of Gaza are often prevented from leaving due to Israeli and Egyptian border restrictions. Infrastructure has crumbled due to wars, artillery exchanges, and the lack of resources to fix them. Gaza is one of the primary humanitarian crises not only in the Middle East, but also in the world. The UN is present in Gaza and provides aid through various channels to citizens who need it. Yet, there are no peacekeeping forces in Gaza. According to the news agency Middle East Monitor, the Israeli government recommended the presence of UN peacekeepers in Gaza – but this proposal was rejected by Hamas (Memo 2017). Thus, the UN is only able to address security concerns in Gaza through a humanitarian approach and not a protective approach.

The United Nations Office for the Coordination of Humanitarian Affairs (OCHA) is present in Gaza. This entity of the UN states that Palestinians living in Gaza are 'locked in' as they face harsh movement restrictions that have intensified since the takeover by Hamas in 2007 (OCHA n.d.). Ongoing tensions between Hamas and the Palestinian Authority (of the West Bank) have led to a dire humanitarian emergency that needs to be urgently addressed to avoid human casualties. In mid-April 2017, the power plant in Gaza stopped operating due to a dispute between Hamas and the Palestinian Authority regarding tax rates for the fuel used for the plant. The resulting fuel and power crisis in Gaza forced the shutdown of hospitals and prevented some citizens living in high-rise buildings access to drinking water. This crisis also transcends the security of the borders of Gaza as the lack of energy to treat raw sewage causes approximately 110 liters of poorly treated sewage to flow into the Mediterranean Sea on a daily basis (OCHA 2017).

Tensions in Gaza have recently reignited, particularly after the United States announced it would move its Embassy to Jerusalem. Beginning in March 2018, Palestinians in Gaza began demonstrating in "the Great March of Return" to mark al-Nakba, or the Catastrophe, in which Palestinians commemorate the mass displacement that occurred due to the war in 1948–

49. The demonstrations, continuing every Friday, resulted in mass violence on 14 May, when at least 60 people were killed and more than 1,300 were injured. Israeli forces used live ammunition, rubber bullets, and tear gas against demonstrators who had assembled along the Gaza–Israel border fence (UN News). The disproportionate use of force against protesters, the majority of which were unarmed, has been condemned. UN Special Coordinator Nickolay Mladenov briefed the Security Council and called for the violence in Gaza to end with the support of the international community, claiming the support would be essential in order to prevent war (UN News 2018). US Ambassador Nikki Haley spoke regarding the matter, claiming that the US Embassy move to Jerusalem reflected "the reality" that it has been the capital of Israel since the founding of the state (UN News 2018). She also claimed that there would be no plausible peace agreement in which Jerusalem was not the capital of Israel – ignoring the fact that predecessors had the negotiation of Jerusalem as a contingent matter of any peace agreement.

It is clear that the UN has a vital role to play in the future of Gaza and Israel. As long as Gaza and Israel continue their tense relationship, the UN needs to continue its active presence. With potential conflict looming, the UN needs to be as proactive as possible in gaining support from the international community to pressure all parties from committing acts of violence and to work towards a peaceful resolution.

Iraq and ISIS

The United Nations Assistance Mission for Iraq (UNAMI) is one of the primary representations of the UN in Iraq. Established in 2003, and greatly expanded in 2007, it remains active today. The UNAMI has a goal that is centered around assisting both the government and people of Iraq and are responsible for numerous initiatives that are critical to promoting increased levels of security. They work with the government and civil society to coordinate humanitarian efforts for UN agencies, funds and programs across the country. The UNAMI does not deliver humanitarian or development programs, but rather it raises the profile for development by engaging in things such as political dialogue, assisting in electoral processes, and facilitating regional dialogue between Iraq and its neighbors.

The UN's role in Iraq is heavily focused on the political realm and humanitarian aid – principally on the refugee or displaced persons population that has grown in the wake of the Islamic State of Iraq and Syria (ISIS). ISIS has occupied territory in Iraq and Syria since 2014 and remained the number one security concern due to its ruthless violence, financial resources, and innovative methods for utilizing social media (Mabon and Stephen 2017). Much UN attention is focused on Mosul following the takeback of the city from ISIS and the level of human rights abuses there becoming evident. In May, the UN refugee agency opened a 12th camp outside of Mosul in order to address the increasing numbers of displaced persons as the prior camp, which is able to house 30,000 people, was full (Gluck 2017). Families that are arriving at the camps report that the situation in Mosul is worsening, with no water, food, fuel, or basic services. Additionally, travelling out of the city in an attempt to reach a camp is a dangerous journey.

The situation in Iraq caused by ISIS is a security concern in several different areas: infrastructure has been destroyed by brutal fighting, hundreds of thousands of people are displaced, and ISIS brutality will have lingering impacts on the people of Iraq. Funding for humanitarian efforts is nowhere near the level it needs to be, with only 17 percent of the $985 million requested by the Humanitarian Response Plan for Iraq coming to fruition (Abdulla 2017). The lack of funding from the international community has the potential to endanger the ability of the UN to properly address the humanitarian crisis which would not help to mitigate security concerns. On top of the necessary basic goods that the UN provides, they are also building field hospitals to assist with victims of trauma (Abdulla 2017). These field hospitals are providing essential services that are necessary for the people of Iraq to have access to after experiencing such high levels of trauma and violence at the hands of ISIS.

During a trip to Baghdad in March 2017, the UN's Secretary-General, António Guterres, pledged to continue the commitment of supplying aid and assisting in rebuilding Iraqi institutions and reiterated the importance that ISIS is held accountable for their human rights abuses – though he was unclear about the role the UN will have in that process (UN News 2017). Even though ISIS appears to have been defeated in Iraq, there is still an ample amount of work for the UN to do in order to help bring security back to the region. Addressing medical needs and providing the citizens methods to deal with the trauma they experienced is a necessary step in bringing security back to the region. Rebuilding infrastructure and political institutions will lead to a stabilization that will also help to increase the level of security. Marta Ruedas, UNDP Resident Representative for Iraq, has pointed out that roads in Iraq are being repaired, hospitals are becoming operational, electricity is being restored, and people are finally able to return to work (United Nations Iraq 2018). She also stated that more than 60 percent of the nearly 6 million displaced people have been able to return home. These are all steps in the right direction, but there is still a large amount that needs to be done before Iraq is once again stable. The international community has a responsibility to provide the necessary aid to the UN to ensure that future stabilization is possible.

The Syrian Civil War and Refugee Crisis

The conflict in Syria that erupted in 2011 has compromised security in the entire country and displaced millions of Syrians. Human rights violations have occurred on large scales during the Syrian crisis and the UN has responded by calling for an "immediate end to violence, the release of political prisoners, impartial investigations to end impunity, ensure accountability and bring perpetrators to justice, and reparations for the victims" (UN News Centre n.d.). Each of these steps are critical in the attempt to restore security to Syria. Since the conflict began, Syria has gone from a middle-income country to one in which four out of five residents live in poverty (UN News Centre n.d.). The displacement of Syrians has also strained the economies of neighboring countries as they attempt to house increasing numbers of Syrian refugees. This also creates an external security concern for these neighboring countries as their own development is being challenged by absorbing large numbers of people that infrastructure and economies are not always equipped to do. The UN addresses this security concern by working to build bridges between humanitarian and development responses to the crisis by supporting increasing the resilience of the most affected communities in both Syria and host countries. They do this by strengthening livelihoods, fostering social cohesion, and rebuilding infrastructure (UN News Centre n.d.).

In December 2014, the UN launched the Regional Refugee and Resilience Plan (3RP) to address the growing concerns in Syria. The 2016–2017 initiative for the 3RP is a combined effort of the UN and more than 200 partners with goals that are not limited to the confines of the Syrian border. Examples of what the 3RP aims to accomplish is creating strong national leadership regarding response planning through the Lebanon Crisis Response Plan, Jordan Response Plan, and 3RP chapters in Turkey, Iraq, and Egypt (3RP Regional Strategic Overview n.d.). It also aims to provide a regional protection framework as well as promote education for young people. One of the most important aspects of security that the 3RP addresses in countries absorbing Syrian refugees is food security – a basic human right that is necessary to be met before other concerns can start to be addressed.

In January 2017, rebel groups and the Syrian government delegation attended talks that were held in Astana, Kazakhstan. This meeting – also attended by Russia, Turkey, Iran, and the UN Special Envoy for Syria – resulted in an agreement of a ceasefire in Syria among the three sponsor countries. In February and March 2017, the Special Envoy convened parties to Geneva for talks that focused on Syria. The topics that were discussed regarded governance, drafting a new constitution, holding elections, and counter-terrorism strategies. These talks continued periodically, either occurring in Geneva or Astana, until the fourth round of Astana talks in early May 2017. The result of the fourth round of Astana talks was the signing of an agreement to create four "de-escalation" zones in Syria, of which the UN Special Envoy stated was a step in a promising direction (UNOG n.d.).

As is evident, the security situation in Syria crosses borders and creates a unique challenge for UN involvement. There are multiple actors that must agree on peace processes while being held accountable for any questionable actions or violations. The UN is involved in the Syrian peace process both by being involved with talks and also by addressing the needs of refugees in both Syria and in host countries. Currently, there are no UN peacekeepers present in Syria. A continuous issue facing UN involvement with Syrian refugees is funding, as is evident by a significant shortfall in a joint UN–EU conference in April 2018. This conference, held in Brussels, had a target of raising $9 billion and ultimately raised only $4 billion. This lack of funding undoubtedly means that some essential UN programs will have to be cut. These funds are also not part of any reconstruction initiatives in Syria, something EU Foreign Affairs Chief Federica Mogherini said would only begin once a peace agreement was in place (Wintour 2018). Funding is necessary for both those in Syria and refugees in countries bordering Syria where tensions are increasing – and at risk of spiraling out of control in places such as Lebanon. What is most evident regarding the relationship between the UN and Syrian refugees is that there will continue to be a desperate need for funding to ensure basic levels of dignity are possible and to ensure basic needs are met.

Yemen

The ongoing civil war in Yemen is one of the most complex issues in the Middle East today. In 2011, the Houthis gained significant power within Yemen as anti-government demonstrations and sentiments spread across the country. By the end of 2011, then President Ali Abdullah Saleh agreed to step down and allow his vice president, Abdrabbuh Mansur Hadi to replace him. Beginning in 2013, the government led by Hadi and opposition groups began the process of engaging in national dialogue, which created a 2014 plan to write a new constitution that would divide Yemen into six provinces. The United Nations was hopeful at this point, with the UN Special Envoy for Yemen claiming that the agreement would lead to democratic governance which would uphold human rights and equal citizenship (Orkaby 2017). Houthi opposition rejected the deal, which can be viewed as a catalyst for what was to come after. Throughout 2014, many Houthis supported anti-government protests that erupted throughout Yemen. In September, the Houthis captured the capital city of Sana'a, which prompted the dissolution of parliament, the forced resignation of Hadi, and a new revolutionary committee that would replace the government

The UN was aware of what was unfolding in Yemen and actively sought to prevent conflict. In February 2015, the UN Security Council demanded Houthi rebels to "immediately and unconditionally" withdraw from all government institutions, release President Hadi, and engage in UN brokered negotiations to work towards democratic transition (United Nations 2015). In March, the Security Council met to address the ongoing crisis. At this meeting, Jamal Benomar, Special Adviser of the Secretary-General on Yemen, expressed his growing concern regarding the growing discontent in Yemen. He stated that he believed the events preceding the meeting were leading Yemen away from peaceful settlement and towards a civil war. Benomar gave detailed accounts during this meeting regarding what was happening on the ground in Yemen. The most notable events were heavy clashes on 19 March between the Central Security Forces and popular committees and bombings that occurred on 20 March in Sana'a, which killed as many as 140 people. He also reported that on 21 and 22 March, Houthi militia and units of the Yemeni army gained control of Taiz, which held geographical significance as the gateway into Aden (Security Council 2015).

The Security Council met again on 14 April to discuss the importance of addressing the escalating situation in Yemen. Topics discussed in this meeting were the emphasis on the potential humanitarian crisis, the importance of human security and human rights, and the issue of Saudi Arabian involvement in the crisis. The Security Council acknowledged that President Hadi had requested the aid of Saudi Arabia, by any means necessary including military-intervention, which is ultimately what happened (Security Council 2015).

This series of events provides a framework for understanding what caused Yemen to become engulfed in a brutal war. It also creates an understanding for the challenges faced by the UN and the Security Council when conflict arises. The Security Council could condemn actions taken by the Houthis and impose sanctions, but the effectiveness of that was limited. At this point, the Houthis were not interested in engaging in democratic peace talks and they did not recognize the legitimacy of President Hadi.

Yemen is one of the greatest security risks in the international community for a multitude of reasons. An estimated 8.3 million people are dependent on external food aid, while 400,000 children are suffering from severe acute malnutrition. Virtually all Yemeni children are in desperate need of humanitarian assistance, which is exemplified by the fact that UNICEF estimates show that 25,000 Yemeni babies have died at birth or before reaching one month (Nehebay 2018). On top of severe food shortages, there are shortages of medical supplies. A diphtheria outbreak quickly spread beginning in December 2017 within areas of Yemen, with nearly 700 cases and 48 associated deaths (Nehebay 2018). Cholera has also been a significant issue in Yemen, with over 1 million cases beginning in early 2017 that have resulted in 2,300 deaths (Yemen Cholera Response 2018). Less than 50% of hospitals across Yemen are operational, 18% of districts have no doctors, and 56% of the population has no regular access to basic healthcare (UN News 2018).

There are currently no UN Peacekeeping forces in Yemen to help ensure that millions of vulnerable people are protected and provided with the aid that they urgently need. The United Nations Development Programme (UNDP) has identified and subsequently constructed a method for addressing some immediate humanitarian concerns, thus hoping to alleviate some of the overall security concerns that this conflict has created. The UNDP is approaching their operations in Yemen from a community-based viewpoint and aims to create programs that will increase the level of resilience. In partnership with the World Bank and USAID, the UNDP has addressed primary needs in 300 out of 333 districts in almost every governorate (Yemen, 2017). One example of an initiative taken on by the UNDP is the creation of Cash for Work (CfW) projects, of which 25,700 people registered for with the result of 12,000 being chosen (Yemen 2017). In 2016, 261 young women were trained as community health or nutrition workers while 800 farmers were identified and financed (Yemen 2017). These programs, along with several others, are conducted in order to encourage economic self-reliance and resilience.

There is also work being done by the UNDP that aims to increase peace-building and governance. These projects or activities are largely funded by individual countries across the world. An example of this is the UNDP NGO Capacity Building Project which trained 66 NGOs on techniques to handle conflict sensitive approaches to providing humanitarian assistance. Several of these were awarded grants in specific governorates which allowed for them to become trusted partners for both the government of Yemen and the international community. There were also efforts to address the human rights violations that have been occurring in Yemen and to provide psychological support to hundreds of victims (Yemen 2017). In January 2017, the UN Special Envoy for Yemen arrived in Aden to meet with key stakeholders in the ongoing conflict. The focus of the meetings was both to renew the cessation of hostilities and to address the increasing humanitarian crisis. The Special Envoy then spent two days in Sana'a to focus on security plans for peace agreements and the need to lift restrictions on civilian aircraft to and from the Sana'a airport (OSESGY 2017).

In April 2017, $1.1 billion for aid to Yemen was pledged at a UN conference in Geneva. However, the situation in Yemen has since worsened. The UN has attempted to address mounting concerns of famine and disease, but the implementation of humanitarian aid is not easily accomplished. In early May 2017, senior UN relief official Jamie McGoldrick called upon all parties involved in the conflict to allow for unrestricted access to citizens across the country (al-Saeed 2017). One of the top concerns and priorities is the allowance of medical supplies and medicine. There have been delays at ports, checkpoints, and interference with other aid delivery that have prevented critical supplies from reaching their destinations (al-Saeed 2017).

Yemen is the greatest concern for human security within the Middle East. If the situation in Yemen does not improve, an additional 10 million people will become food insecure by the end of this year (UN News 2018). While the UN does not provide peacekeepers to aid in mitigating conflict, it does provide essential services for promoting peace building that leads to a higher level of human security. The challenge for the UN in Yemen is getting all parties involved to cooperate for the benefit of the civilians, or the most vulnerable population. This has consistently proven to be incredibly difficult, especially given direct Saudi military involvement in the conflict. The UN consistently attempts to provide essential humanitarian aid, build economic self-reliance and resilience, and implement vital social services that are necessary for the betterment of human security.

Conclusion

In April 2017, the UN Special Coordinator for the Middle East Peace Process, Nickolay Mladenov, addressed the Security Council regarding the fragile state of the Middle East. He stated that 'a perfect storm has engulfed the Middle East and continues to threaten international peace and security' (Romenzi 2017). Mladenov noted that the instability has paved the way for foreign intervention and manipulation which could ultimately create more instability. Most importantly, he also addressed explicitly that the situations taking place in the Middle East create social exclusion or marginalized populations, which both can provide grounds for an increase of violent extremism.

The UN recognizes that there needs to be unity across every ethnic and religious line to continue addressing the situation in the Middle East. The conflicts currently facing the Middle East have created the largest refugee crisis since the Second World War and this population of vulnerable people create a difficult challenge for neighboring countries attempting to aid them (Romenzi 2017). The level of human suffering in the Middle East increases the concern over security in a multitude of ways, such as the exploitation of vulnerable populations or the lack of resources being provided to address basic health care and trauma. The UN needs the continuing support of the international community in order to continue their humanitarian and protective missions in the Middle East. Failing to garner the support of the international community could prove to be detrimental to the security of the Middle East in the coming years.

The UN will need to remain in the Middle East for the foreseeable future. With the presence of ISIS winding down, the war in Yemen, the conflict between Israelis and Palestinians, and with other regional issues, the UN is able to fill the role of a moderating third party. The UN is also providing critical support to the people in areas that are subject to degrading and dehumanizing conditions every day. However, as an institution of global governance, the UN cannot continue operating at its current capacity in the Middle East without unwavering support of the international community. If anything, key actors that are involved with the Middle East should be doing more to support UN efforts, be it financially or by other means. As time progresses the UN should attempt to involve regional actors, such as the Arab League, more often in attempt to decrease their role in governance. The Arab League has been involved, but it appears as though this involvement has been limited. Given that the Arab League is a prominent regional organization in the Middle East, they need to be given a more active platform and presence with the UN. Doing so is necessary to both create and promote any possibilities for peace and stability.

References

n.d. *3RP Regional Strategic Overview.* http://www.3rpsyriacrisis.org/wp-content/uploads/2015/12/3RP-Regional-Overview-2016-2017.pdf.

Abdulla, Ivan. 2017. *UN News.* April 26. http://www.un.org/apps/news/story.asp?NewsID=56631#.WRng0WgrLIU.

al-Saeed, K. (2017, May 8). *UN News.* Retrieved from Unimpeded access, humanitarian funds urgently needed in Yemen – senior UN relief official: https://news.un.org/en/story/2017/05/556802-unimpeded-access-humanitarian-funds-urgently-needed-yemen-senior-un-relief#.WRiT8GgrLIU

Coker, Margaret, and Falih Hassan. 2017. "The New York Times." *Iraq Prime Minister Declares Victory Over ISIS.* Dec 9. https://www.nytimes.com/2017/12/09/world/middleeast/iraq-isis-haider-al-abadi.html.

Delpech, Therese. 2006. *Iran and the Bomb.* Paris: Editions Autrement.

Gama, C. F. (2009). Bridge Over Troubled Waters: United Nations, Peace Operations and Human Security. *Journal of Human Security*, 9-31.

Gluck, Caroline. 2017. *UN News.* May 12. https://news.un.org/en/story/2017/05/557202-iraq-un-refugee-agency-opens-twelfth-camp-displacement-escalates-west-mosul#.WRnguGgrLIU.

Human Rights Watch. February 14. https://www.hrw.org/news/2017/02/14/lebanon-new-refugee-policy-step-forward.

Hussain, Nazir, and Sannia Abdullah. 2015. "Iran Nuclear Deal: Implications for Regional Security." *Journal of Political Studies,* 22 (2): 479–493.

Khan, Saira. 2010. *Iran and Nuclear Weapons: Protracted conflict and proliferation.* New York: Routledge.

Mabon, Simon, and Royle Stephen. 2017. *The Origins of ISIS: The Collapse of Nations and Revolution in the Middle East.* London: L.B. Tauris & Co Ltd.

Mehta, Rupal N., and Rachel Elizabeth Whitlark. 2016. "Unpacking the Iranian Nuclear Deal: Nuclear Latency and US Foreign Policy." *The Washington Quarterly,* 39 (4): 45–61.

2017. *Memo.* February 28. https://www.middleeastmonitor.com/20170228-hamas-rejects-israeli-idea-for-un-peacekeepers-in-gaza/.

Mohammed, Arshad. 2017. *US lawmakers aim to comply with Iran nuclear deal: EU.* November 7. http://www.reuters.com/article/us-iran-nuclear-mogherini/u-s-lawmakers-aim-to-comply-with-iran-nuclear-deal-eu-idUSKBN1D72AY.

Nebehay, S. (2018). *Reuters.* Retrieved from U.N. hopes imports will help stave off famine in Yemen as diphtheria spreads: https://www.reuters.com/article/us-yemen-security-un/u-n-hopes-imports-will-help-stave-off-famine-in-yemen-as-diphtheria-spreads-idUSKBN1F516M

n.d. *OCHA.* https://www.ochaopt.org/location/gaza-strip.

2017. *OCHA*. April 27. https://www.ochaopt.org/content/un-coordinator-humanitarian-aid-and-development-activities-releases-emergency-funding-fuel.

2017. *OCHA*. May 19. https://www.ochaopt.org/content/statement-humanitarian-coordinator-robert-piper-electricity-crisis-gaza.

Orkaby, A. (2017). Yemen's Humanitarian Nightmare: The Real Roots of the Conflict. *Foreign Affairs, 96*(6), 93–101.

OSESGY. (2017, January 16). Retrieved from The UN Special Envoy for Yemen Arrives to Aden: https://osesgy.unmissions.org/un-special-envoy-yemen-arrives-aden

OSESGY. (2017, January 23). Retrieved from UN Envoy for Yemen Concludes Visit to Sana'a: https://osesgy.unmissions.org/un-envoy-yemen-concludes-visit-sanaa

Pokharel, Tilak. 2016. *UNIFIL.* Oct 3. https://unifil.unmissions.org/lebanese-soldiers-join-un-peacekeepers-peace-relay-march.

2015. Resolution 2231, UN. http://www.un.org/en/sc/2231/.

Roehrlich, Elisabeth. 2016. "The Cold War, the developing world, and the creation of the International Atomic Energy Agency." *Cold War History* 16 (2): 195–212.

Romenzi, Alessio. 2017. *UN News.* April 20. https://news.un.org/en/story/2017/04/555662-middle-east-engulfed-perfect-storm-one-threatens-international-peace-warns-un#.WR-OCGgrLIU.

Samore, Gary. 2015. *The Iran Nuclear Deal: A Definitive Guide.* Belfer Center for Science and International Affairs, Harvard Kennedy School, Cambridge: President and Fellows of Harvard College.

Security Council. (2015, March 22). Retrieved from 7411th Meeting: http://www.un.org/en/ga/search/view_doc.asp?symbol=S/PV.7411

Security Council. (2015, April 14). Retrieved from 7426th Meeting: http://www.un.org/en/ga/search/view_doc.asp?symbol=S/PV.7426

2017. *Tripartite*. April 20. https://unifil.unmissions.org/unifil-head-chairs-regular-tripartite-meeting-laf-and-idf-officials.

United Nations. (2015, February 15). Retrieved from With Yemen Gripped in Crisis, Security Council Coalesces around Resolution 2201 (2015) Demanding Houthis Withdrawal from Government Institutions: https://www.un.org/press/en/2015/sc11781.doc.htm

UN News. (2016, May 21). Retrieved from http://www.un.org/apps/news/story.asp?NewsID=54007#.WjvKxd-nHIU

2017. *UN News*. March 2. http://www.un.org/apps/news/story.asp?NewsID=56272#.WR9-DWgrLIU.

2017. UN News. March 30. http://www.un.org/apps/news/story.asp?NewsID=56465#.WRnvo2grLIU.

2016. *UN News*. May 21. http://www.un.org/apps/news/story.asp?NewsID=54007#.WjvKxd-nHIU.

2018. "UN News." Security Council calls for calm following deadly Gaza clashes; diplomats debate US embassy move. May 15. https://news.un.org/en/story/2018/05/1009792.

UN News. (2018). Retrieved from Yemen: https://news.un.org/en/focus/yemen

UN News. (2018, May 24). Retrieved from Yemen: Human suffering at risk of further deterioration, warns UN aid chief: https://news.un.org/en/story/2018/05/1010651

n.d. *United Nations*. Retrieved from Charter of the United Nations: http://www.un.org/en/sections/un-charter/chapter-i/index.html

n.d. *UN News Centre*. http://www.un.org/apps/news/infocusRel.asp?infocusID=146.

n.d. *UNHCR*. http://reporting.unhcr.org/node/2520#_ga=2.243109633.20243646.1495141721-1178618403.1494353381.

n.d. *UNIFIL Background*. https://unifil.unmissions.org/unifil-background#Para1.

n.d. *UNIFIL Civil Interaction.* https://unifil.unmissions.org/unifil-civil-interaction.

n.d. *UNIFIL Fact Sheet.* https://peacekeeping.un.org/en/mission/unifil.

n.d. *UNIFIL Operations.* https://unifil.unmissions.org/unifil-operations.

United Nations Development Programme. 2017. "UNDP Results Yemen." April. http://www.ye.undp.org/content/yemen/en/home/library/general/results-2016.html.

n.d. *United Nations Iraq.* http://www.uniraq.com/index.php?option=com_k2&view=item&layout=item&id=943&Itemid=637&lang=en.

"United Nations Iraq." 2018. Australia substantially increases support to stabilization in Iraq. May 11. http://www.uniraq.org/index.php?option=com_k2&view=item&id=9055:australia-substantially-increases-support-to-stabilization-in-iraq&Itemid=605&lang=en.

n.d. *UNOG.* https://www.unog.ch/unog/website/news_media.nsf/(httpPages)/E409A03F0D7CFB4AC1257F480045876E?OpenDocument..

n.d. *UNOG.* https://www.unog.ch/unog/website/news_media.nsf/%28httpPages%29/4d6470dbeaf92917c1257e59004fac2d?OpenDocument.

Weiss, T. G. (2016). *What's Wrong with the United Nations and How to Fix It.* Cambridge: Polity Press.

Wintour, Patrick. 2018. "The Guardian." *Donor conference for Syrian refugees falls $5bn short of UN target.* April 25. https://www.theguardian.com/world/2018/apr/25/un-eu-conference-syrian-aid.

Yemen. (2017, May 1). Retrieved from UNDP Yemen Results 2016: http://www.ye.undp.org/content/yemen/en/home/library/general/results-2016.html

Yemen Cholera Response. (2018, July 07). Retrieved from Weekly Epidemiological Bulliten: http://www.emro.who.int/images/stories/yemen/week_26.pdf?ua=1

9

Hegemonic Aspirations and Middle East Discord: The Case of Iran

ALI G. DIZBONI & SOFWAT OMAR

A Gramscian concept at birth, hegemony entered the IR field through efforts to contest the Classical Realist definition of power. Authors of a neoliberal persuasion such as Robert Keohane and Joseph Nye conceived of hegemony as a mixture of hard and soft power. Post-WWII United States (US) hegemony served as a textbook case for such a conception. Use of the concept of hegemony about rising regional powers is relative but refers to their potential capacity to influence the regional or international system by exploiting regional power vacuums (instabilities and crises), by combining the material and non-material powers of the state and reaching out to develop extra-regional alliances. The regional discord resulting from the breakup of the Taliban and Saddam Hussein regimes, along with the Arab Spring and the ensuing sectarian-ethnic civil wars in various states have created opportunities for resourceful revisionist states such as Iran to seek greater influence and to extend their strategic depth at the expense of smaller, yet rich, status quo oil exporting Arab monarchies.

Iranian influence has been growing rapidly in the Middle East ever since two anti-Iranian regimes in Afghanistan and Iraq fell in 2001 and 2003. Increasing US military presence in the neighborhood pushed Iran to shift its (formal) policy of non-alignment to gain full membership of the Shanghai Cooperation Organization (SCO), and to grow closer to both Russia and China (Dizboni, Haji-Yousefi, and Mcpherson 2010). This has allowed Iran to gain new economic opportunities, trading partners, and powerful partners in the international arena. Nevertheless, the Multilateral Security Council sanctions against Iran due to its nuclear program, in addition to previous US sanctions in place since 1979, have devastated the Iranian economy, causing problems such as hyperinflation, depreciation of the Iranian currency, and massive unemployment. After analyzing the Iranian situation, it is important to determine whether Iran can be classified as both a rising and a regional power; either a rising or a regional power; or neither a rising or a regional power.

Although there is no definite, standardized definition for the phrase, "rising power," it is most commonly described as a state that is drastically improving its economic capabilities. For example, according to a report that was drafted by Goldman Sachs, a rising power is one that has "the potential to reshape the global economic and political landscape of the twenty-first century" (Hart and Jones 2011). While most analysts claim that members of the BRICS nations – Brazil, Russia, India, China, and South Africa – are the primary candidates to be classified as a "rising power," some state that Iran may also be included in that group. After all, unlike before, a multi-polar world is present today, where the post-Cold War unipolar order is being increasingly contested by a multipolar economic order. According to Wolhfort, whose work focuses primarily on realist theories, "a multipolar world can be the result of the emergence of regional [powers] that can build coalitions to counter the superpower" (Wolhfort 1991). Since developing countries do not necessarily have the ability to challenge the international system, for instance by not having enough influence in the IMF or the UN Security Council, they seek to gain alliances with more powerful states and transform themselves into "power poles of a future multipolar system" (Flems 2007). This is exactly what Iran has done. Iran's continuous attempts to look East, towards both China and Russia, along with its economic policy of *neither East nor West* may be interpreted as their attempts to challenge the current international system. Iran has attempted to alter its foreign policy of neutrality "to pursue benefits from extensive security-economic cooperation between itself and Shanghai Cooperation Organization (SCO) nation states" (Dizboni, Haji-Yousefi, Mcpherson 2010).

Rising Power

Before analyzing whether Iran qualifies as a rising power, it is important to understand what the phrase "rising power" truly means. Interestingly there are four major features of any rising power, and they include a growing economy, an international recognition of a particular state's growing power, the increasing ability of a state to project soft power on other states, and the capability to challenge the status quo. Other features that may also be attributed to rising powers are a strong military with substantial political power resources, a certain amount of internal cohesion to maintain stability, and an increasingly influential role in international organizations (Tank 2013). Furthermore, a rising power may have the potential to create new regional groups, or significantly influence any existing one, such as the SCO. It normally seeks to create a more multipolar world, one where the post-Second World War order is continuously challenged. A rising power usually seeks positive relations with other powers, to bolster its economy, security, and influence in the international arena. Last but not least, it is usually distinct from middle powers, such as Canada, because unlike such middle powers, they did not fully integrate into the post-1945 world order, which led to a heavy conditioning of "their strategic interests and conceptions of national purpose" (Hurrell 2006).

Regional Power

Although regional powers share some common attributes with rising powers, the two are still distinct. Regional powers, also referred to as regional leaders or local powers, are states that have a significant influence only in their respective geographical location. Consequently, Samuel Huntington once defined regional powers as countries that are "pre-eminent in [particular] areas of the world, without being able to extend their interest as globally as the United States" (Huntington 1999). As indicated by another researcher, there are three main general features of all regional powers, and they include: (1) being part of a particular geographical area of a delineated region; (2) having the capacity to counter any aggressive actions from neighboring unfriendly states; and (3) maintaining a strong influence across the entire region (Osterud 2007). In addition, they are distinguishable from rising powers and middle powers (such as Canada) also due to them having a claim to leadership, the presence of power resources, the employment of foreign policy instruments, and the acceptance of leadership (Flems 2007).

Iran: Rising but Fragile

Iran meets many of the requirements of a rising, regional power. It is a member of a delineated region, one where it can counter any aggressive behavior from neighboring unfriendly states. For example, even though there is a fierce competition with Saudi Arabia to become the regional hegemon, Iran still manages to remain influential and can negate any aggression from its Arab neighbors. Nevertheless, although Iran possesses a greater number of land forces and a vibrant defense industry where it manufactures many of its own weapons, its military is still less technologically advanced or equipped than some of its neighbors', such as Turkey, Israel, and Saudi Arabia. This is not surprising, considering that Turkey is a NATO member, and both Saudi Arabia and Israel receive some of the world's most advanced weaponry from the United States of America. Despite having a less technologically advanced military, Iran has still proved its ability to develop missile technology and to threaten, intimidate, and carry out low-intensity attacks – directly or through the use of proxy groups – against both major and regional powers. Therefore, Iran is highly influential in Middle Eastern politics, and is the center of gravity of the Shia Crescent, which also comprises Syria, Iraq, Lebanon, Yemen, and Bahrain. Iran tends to view itself as the guardian of Shia Islam, and openly supports other state and non-state actors that serve its interests in a strategic manner.

Iran's quest for regional hegemony is simple and clear. Unlike some of its neighbors, it possesses internal stability, which consists of relative vertical (national political community) and horizontal (leadership) homogeneity combined with hybrid features of vibrant electoral and political Islam (Buzan 2016). It also has enormous economic potential, due to the gradual relaxation of international sanctions and its vast quantities of natural resources. Iran maintains a strategic stretch to Iraq, Syria, Yemen, Lebanon, and Bahrain, based on common Shia networks and common interests. In addition, in order to receive international support, it has strongly aligned itself with Russia and China, both of whom are permanent members of the United Nations Security Council. For instance, this cooperation with the two great powers can be seen in Syria, where Russian airstrikes are supporting Iranian, Syrian, and Hezbollah forces, and also in the joint military maneuvers with China. There has been a peaceful solution to Iran's right to peaceful enrichment, despite strong opposition from some regional states, such as Israel and Saudi Arabia, and the Republicans in the United States. Due to Iranian diplomacy with the outside world, there has been a prospect for normalization, both in terms of Iran's economy and US–EU–Iranian relations. As a result, Iran had the ability to snatch mitigated victory from the jaws of defeat.

Although there are promising signs for Iran following a diplomatic solution to the nuclear negotiations, some analysts still suggest that Iran has a failed foreign policy and that it deals from a position of weakness (Juneau 2014). According to Juneau, although Iran possesses a large educated population, a central geographic location with strategic interests, and enormous amounts of natural resources, Iran's power is still weak due to poor military capabilities, mismanagement of the economy, and corruption. As a result, Iran's influence in the Middle East is diminishing rapidly (Juneau 2014).

Juneau argues that the Iranian Armed Forces have outdated weapons that do not pose any threat in the 21st century. Due to the low reliability and inefficiency of Iranian weaponry, Iran primarily has unconventional capabilities, where it is able to use proxy groups across the Middle Eastern region to interfere and disrupt the internal affairs of neighboring states. Although these assets do allow Iran to deter potential threats, they usually do not result in any form of confrontation. As a result, these major problems may not get solved in the near future, due to the combination of economic constraints, years of underinvestment, and incompetence of the Iranian regime (Juneau 2017).

Iran's Economic Capabilities

Iran possesses a lot of natural resources. However, its crude oil exports have been under severe international sanctions due to its nuclear program. (With the current removal, however fragile, of these nuclear sanctions, the economy shows relative rising growth in GDP) Once these sanctions are removed, the Iranian economy is expected to rise rapidly. This will, in turn, result in a higher GDP in the future. This trend towards a stronger, more diversified economy is reflected in the 2015 IMF report on the Iran, it states:

> […] the JCPOA is expected to provide relief from sanctions in four broad areas: (1) export and transportation of hydrocarbon and hydrocarbon-related products; (2) banking and other financial services and transactions, including restored access to the international payment system (SWIFT); (3) access to foreign financial assets; and (4) the sale, supply of parts, and transfer of goods and services to the automotive and air transportation sectors, and associated foreign investment. The sanctions relief will bring three key benefits for Iran. First and foremost, it will be a positive *external demand shock*, both for oil and non-oil exports. In addition, the decline in the cost of external trade and financial transactions will act as a positive *terms-of-trade shock* (lowering the price of imports and raising the price of exports). Finally, restored access to foreign assets and higher oil exports should also result in a positive *wealth effect* (IMF 2016).

In addition to the report by the IMF, the Intelligence Unit from the Economist also provides useful information about the Iranian economy. It states that "with the prospect of sanctions being lifted from 2016, notably on oil exports and the banking sector, the economy will witness a more rapid recovery even with low oil prices" (EIU Digital Solutions 2018). See *Annex A* for a forecast summary for Iran's economy from 2015–2020. Furthermore, it is predicted that Iran will have the fastest growth in the Middle East and North African Region from 2016–2020, due to the combination of Iran's hydrocarbons wealth, demographics and economic diversity, and the removal of international sanctions. See *Annex B* for Iran's economic growth in both the private and the public sector. Iran also boasts a sizable population compared to its neighboring states, which in turn results in a higher amount of domestic consumption. With a large pool of labor, and an educated population, Iran is poised to grow economically every year, as seen in *Annex C*. The decrease in inflation since the start of President Rouhani's tenure, combined with a more sustainable trade balance and a diversification of trade partners, allow room for more optimism in the Iranian economy (See *Annex D*). A comparison with neighboring Arab countries, especially with the members of the GCC, provides an accurate representation of Iran's comparative economic indicators, and this can be found in *Annex E* (EIU Digital Solutions 2018).

Iran's Regional Ties and Networks

Iran's involvement in the Lebanon hostage crisis, unwavering support to Hezbollah, a declaratory anti-Israel policy, and the ongoing nuclear program provide the context for assessing the neoclassical realism theory for explaining Iranian foreign policy.

The Lebanon hostage crisis lasted from the early 1980s to 1992. The hostages were mostly foreign citizens from Europe and America. They were abducted by an organization called Islamic Jihad that was closely affiliated with Hezbollah (Ranstorp 1997). The Iranian regime strongly supports Hezbollah in Lebanon. Before the establishment of Hezbollah, allies of Ayatollah Khomeini trained with Shia paramilitary organizations in Lebanon and Syria in the early 1970s (Ma'oz 2004). After the Iranian Revolution of 1979, Hezbollah was formed in 1982 (Levitt 2013). Thus, the new Iranian government successfully established unprecedented levels of cooperation with Lebanese Shia militias.

Ironically, Israel secretly supplied weapons to Iran's theocratic regime during the Iraq–Iran war (Parsi 2007). Iran was badly in need of weaponry, and the Israeli government covertly supplied US-made weapons (Walsh 2018). Besides anti-Israel rhetoric, Iranian activity against Israel was limited primarily to strategic military targets until the early 1990s (Bayman 2007). Starting from 1992, Iran softened its policy of exporting the Shia revolution in favor of standing up against Western governments and Israel (Bayman 2007).

Iran's nuclear development program was long suspected during the 1990s (Tayekh 2005). However, when details of an enrichment facility at Natanz and a heavy water facility at Arak were disclosed by an Iranian dissident group in 2002, calls were made for an immediate halt to the Iranian nuclear program (CFR 2018). The subsequent negotiations addressed the widespread concerns over Iran's obligations as a signatory to the Non-Proliferation Treaty (NPT) (Ansari 2007).

Neoclassical realism provides a credible explanation for Iranian foreign policy from 1979 to the present day. This variant of Realist theory argues that the international system "provides incentives for states to emulate the successful political, military, and technological practices of the system's leading states or to counter such practices through innovation" (Taliaferro 2006). In addition, neoclassical realism also explains the "foreign policies of states in specific contexts taking into consideration the internal differences of the states under scrutiny, which can be due to material factors (e.g. military or economic power) or to non-material issues (such as norms or perceptions)" (Costalli 2009).

The balance of threat is an important concept while analyzing the Iranian foreign policy. When a state feels threatened by another nation's superior power, it seeks to balance the threats by allying itself with other states or militia groups. Although a state has a greater potential to threaten others by having a "greater share of total resources (population, industrial/military capabilities, technological prowess) ... the level of threat that a state imposes is not just based solely on the distribution of that power (i.e. foreign influence and political penetration)" (Watson 2001). Other factors, including "geographic proximity, offensive power, and aggressive intentions affect" the level of threat a particular state poses (Watson 2001).

Neoclassical realism explains the Iranian participation in the Lebanon Hostage Crisis by addressing Iran's asymmetric approach to balance regional threats. These threats are primarily from Israel and America. By using Western hostages as a proxy, Iran strategically defeated the Multinational Force in Lebanon (or MNF), which was strongly supported by the US (Pollack 2005). The abduction of Western citizens using a subservient militia group in Lebanon also allowed Iran to maintain a credible deniability of its involvement. Furthermore, the Iranian influence on Hezbollah was also instrumental in brokering arms-for-hostages deals with the US and gaining concessions from France and Germany (Grubb 2010). With an ongoing war in Iraq during the 1980s, the Iranian regime desperately needed new weapons (Parsi 2007). Once it was exposed that Iran was indirectly responsible for the abduction of hostages, the Iranian government continued to seek further deals involving arms-for-hostages swaps (Limbert 2009). This quest for desperately needed weapons is best explained by neoclassical realism.

Iran's quest to become the undisputed regional power can also be seen in its attempt to support Bashar al-Assad, the current ruler of Syria. Iran has made many strategic allies to support its military operations, even though Arab and Western countries have continued to support different groups that are opposed to the present Syrian government. The Syrian civil war started during the spring of 2011 when many Syrians protested against the government of Syrian President Bashar al-Assad. Following these protests turned into armed rebellion, the Syrian government initiated a crackdown that eventually transformed into a large-scale civil war between many different actors, primarily the armed rebels and the pro-government forces (BBC 2018).

Although the Syrian civil war may seem to be a domestic issue, it actually involves many different actors. Supporters of Bashar al-Assad's regime include Hezbollah and Iran. Furthermore, in the United Nations Security Council, Russia and China have continuously supported Syria. The Russians have a military installation in the naval port of Tartus, Syria. It is in a very strategic location since it is their only Mediterranean port that has the capability of ship maintenance and repair work. Furthermore, by maintaining a port at Tartus, the Russian Navy saves time. This is because, without the naval facility in Tartus, Russian warships would have been forced to travel back to the Black Sea via the Turkish Straits for any maintenance and repair work. Similarly, the Chinese government also supports the Syrian government due to its policy of non-intervention in the affairs of other states. In addition, Russia and China, both authoritarian states themselves, are "concerned about the way repressive regimes have been falling in the Arab Spring" (Grammaticas 2018). Fighting against the Syrian government are various rebel groups.

The rebel groups who are fighting against the Syrian government are supported by major Middle Eastern states including Qatar, Turkey, and Saudi Arabia. Furthermore, the Senate of the United States has recently passed a bill that supports the arming and finance of various Syrian rebel groups (Roberts 2018). Nevertheless, it is difficult to manage the different rebel groups.

The rebel groups against Bashar al-Assad are not united. They come from various backgrounds. While some are moderate, the most powerful ones are Islamic extremists. For example, one of the most prominent rebel groups is the al-Nusra Front, and they are an offshoot of al-Qaeda. Furthermore, another rebel group, ISIS (also known as the Islamic State and ISIL), are so violent that they have been disowned by al-Qaeda. Due to a lack of organization and inadequate capabilities, the moderate rebel groups have little power and influence. In contrast, fundamentalist groups, such as the al-Nusra Front, are well funded and they possess a wide array of advanced military hardware – including weapons that have been stolen from other groups (Friedman and Siemaszko 2018).

Although arming and financing the moderate Syrian rebel groups may seem like an appealing strategy, in theory, it is quite unrealistic and impractical. The fundamentalist rebel groups have seized advanced weaponry from other groups. Due to their generous funding, many fighters from more moderate groups have switched their allegiance and joined the extremists. Therefore, there is a very high probability that any funding or weapons from Western states would eventually reach the wrong recipients and indirectly support violent extremist groups (Allott 2014).

Advanced weaponry from the United States has already reached the Islamic State (IS). When IS fighters ransacked the Iraqi city of Mosul, the Iraqi Army quickly surrendered, left their American weapons, and fled south towards Baghdad. These sophisticated weapons were soon confiscated by fundamentalist rebels. A similar event may take place in Syria if Western states arm and fund any rebel group (Crowley *et al.* 2014). The end result will undoubtedly be costly, since the entire Middle Eastern region is experiencing hostilities between people from different religious and cultural backgrounds.

The conflict in Syria is also a battle between Sunni and Shia Islam. Bashar al-Assad and his family belong to the Alawite sect of Shiism. Similarly, Hezbollah and Iran are comprised mainly of Shia soldiers as well. In contrast, the rebels and their Gulf state supporters are primarily Sunnis. The al-Nusra Front, the Islamic State, and the Saudis, in particular, are adherents of the very strict Hanbali interpretation of Islam. Therefore, with deep sectarian divisions, the Syrian civil war has attracted fighters from all corners of the Muslim world. The conflict between Sunnis and Shias is over 14 centuries old, and it is unlikely to end anytime soon. With so many actors playing a critical role, introducing more weapons into this already destructive conflict will simply worsen the situation (Ruys 2014).

Neoclassical realism explains the unwavering Iranian support to Hezbollah and the Syrian government by highlighting Iran's quest for exporting its theological revolution and to extend its strategic and security depth. Exporting the revolution of 1979 to other countries in the region would allow Iran to counter the influence of Israel, the United States, and other Sunni-dominated Arab regimes. In turn, Iran would rise, and this would inevitably cause a "Shia revival" (Nasr 2007). Furthermore, a "cursory analysis of demographic trends illustrates that long-term alliance with Israel is less likely to ensure Iran's security than multiple alliances with Arab states" (Grubb 2010). Therefore, Iran strategically redefined the basis for regional alliances "regarding religion (as opposed to ethnicity)" and advertised the importance of an Islamic alliance against Israeli and Western forces (Grubb 2010).

According to neoclassical realism, the Iranian quest for a nuclear program derives from Iranian national security concerns. Before 2003, the threats from Iraq provoked the Iranians to embark upon a nuclear program. Memories of Saddam Hussain's use of chemical weapons during the Iraq–Iran war were still fresh, and many Iranians believed that a nuclear program would act as a strategic deterrent against potential enemies (Grubb 2010). Furthermore, the Iranian government does not trust Western states, particularly the United States of America. This is because prior to the Iranian Revolution of 1979, the US strongly supported the Shah who was vehemently pro-Western and threatened the interests of the Iranian clergy (Niklos 1983). In addition, CIA agents also deposed the democratically elected PM of Iran, Mohammed Mosaddegh, in 1953, and subsequently re-established the dictatorship of the Shah (Daneshvar 1996). These actions by the US have forced the Iranian government to desperately ensure its survival by any means.

With few allies in the international stage, Iran must look out for itself and assume the worst. Thus, it routinely helps the Shia militia group Hezbollah and seeks material power and capabilities to survive in an uncertain and anarchic world. Due to the ongoing Saudi–Iranian rivalry for regional hegemony and an anti-Israel stance, Iran experiences a security dilemma. The uncertainty of the Middle East provides an incentive for Iran to acquire sophisticated military capabilities and to increase its power. Thus, over the years, Iran has gradually spent more money on its national defense. Although a particular state may seek military capabilities for only defensive purposes, other states may interpret it as a threat and in turn, enhance their own militaries. This dynamic has triggered an arms race in the Middle East.

The main actors in the inter-state level of analysis are Israel, United States of America, and Saudi Arabia. The main objective of these three states is to act as the regional hegemon, and this subsequently threatens Iran's quest for regional hegemony and poses a security threat to Iran. Furthermore, international sanctions by Western nations, particularly the US, have crippled the Iranian economy by hampering Iran's GDP growth, raising inflation, and decreasing oil production levels. The Iranian government, therefore, seeks to negotiate with the international community to ensure the prosperity of Iran.

Neoclassical realism provides a credible explanation on why Iran behaves the way it does. Iran faces increasing threats from other states, particularly Israel, the United States of America, and Saudi Arabia. The inter-state level conflicts have forced the Iranian regime to ensure its survival by any means. Thus, although Iran faces many economic challenges, it still invests substantial resources to strengthen its military. The Iranian involvement in the Lebanon Hostage Crisis, support to Hezbollah, anti-Israel policy, and the ongoing nuclear program provide the context for assessing the neoclassical realism theory for explaining Iranian foreign policy.

Iran's Aspirations, Extra-regional Alliances and the Shanghai Cooperation Organization

Although the Iranian government initially had a foreign policy of non-alignment towards Western and Eastern powers since the Iranian Revolution of 1979, it eventually changed its foreign policy after thirty years for two primary reasons. Firstly, although healthy relations with both China and Russia had already existed, the failure of moderate President Khatami (1997–2005) in rapprochement with the US, highlighted by George W. Bush's infamous speech on the Axis of Evil, accelerated the rise of neoconservatives in Iran. Furthermore, perhaps more significantly, stronger ties with Russia and China allowed Iran to achieve its security needs through the SCO. Thus, by having healthy relations with neighboring SCO states, Iran believes that its SCO partners would never take a neutral stand and would instead support Iran at all costs in the international arena should its security and stability come under serious threat (Brummer 2007).

By having a foreign policy that maintains close ties with both Russia and China, there may be enormous political and economic opportunities for Iran. Since a diplomatic solution to the Iranian Nuclear Program has been achieved against all the odds, full membership into the SCO, as opposed to being an observer state, may also dramatically alter the world's energy balance of power. For example, the amount of natural gas in the SCO zone would be almost 50% of the world's total reserves, and the amount of oil would increase to roughly 20% (Brummer 2007). At the same time, different sources of renewable energy, such as solar power, are becoming increasingly popular. As a result, the power of O.P.E.C. would undoubtedly decline, since it would be more difficult for them to set prices, production targets, and the overall stability of the global energy market. With close military and economic ties with both Russia and China, Iran seeks to gain permanent SCO membership and greater bargaining power while negotiating with the EU and the US (Vakil 2006). Fortunately for Iran, both Russia and China have indicated that they support Iran's full inclusion into the SCO, following the removal of international sanctions. Keen to highlight itself as a rising regional power, the Iranian regime explicitly states the importance of the SCO. They believe that joining the organization is an act of defiance emphasized when the US sought to join the SCO as an observer state in 2005 but was unilaterally rejected.

Iran, therefore, believes that the SCO is a mechanism against American hegemony (Ehteshami 2009).

Iran is able to meet two strategic objectives via the SCO. Firstly, by joining the SCO, it will stop its international isolation and better manage its tense relations with the West. Since both India and Pakistan will become full members of the SCO from 2016 on, Iran also seeks to follow them and become a full member as soon as possible (PTI 2015). Thus, Iran will be in a prime position to bargain with the organization's two main members, Russia and China, for support in the international arena and security against any threat. Furthermore, joining the SCO will result in greater support for Iran's Nuclear Program, since both Russia and China are not only partners in technology, but also in the realm of international relations, where they are able to use their veto power in the UN Security Council to protect Iranian interests. Due to a diplomatic solution to Iran's Nuclear Program, Iran now has no obstacles to upgrading from an observer state to a full member of the SCO, which in turn will increase Iran's power both regionally and globally.

Conclusion

A "rising power" is one that is rising economically, and its power is recognized by other states. They also project soft power and could change the status quo. A "regional power" is one that is located in a geographically defined region, is able to counter any coalition of surrounding states, and plays an influential role in regional affairs. An Iranian nuclear agreement is an economic game changer, providing global investors access to one of the most promising markets in the developing world. Iran's economy, which is already improving rapidly, will continue to grow once sanctions are eased. Iran plays a major role in regional issues and will continue to do so in order to protect or uphold the safety and security of the Shia Crescent. It is increasingly becoming the regional hegemon. Iran's military capabilities act as an effective deterrent against enemy forces, and will likely increase once the sanctions are fully removed. Iran, therefore, is, in fact, a rising regional power today.

Annexes

Annex A

Forecast Summary of the Iranian Economy from 2015–2020 (Solutions, EIU Digital 2018)

(% unless otherwise indicated)

	2015[a]	2016[b]	2017[b]	2018[b]	2019[b]	2020[b]
Real GDP growth	1.4	6.1	6.0	5.3	5.2	5.5
Crude oil production ('000 b/d)	2,862	3,349	3,416	3,477	3,547	3,671
Oil exports (US$ m)	44,705	63,153	74,915	82,686	85,015	89,367
Consumer price inflation (av)	14.7	14.0	13.6	12.7	11.5	11.9
Consumer price inflation (end-period)	14.0	13.4	13.1	12.0	11.2	12.0
1-year deposit rate	16.0	16.0	14.5	13.0	13.0	14.0
Official net budget balance (% of GDP)	-3.1	-2.3	-2.5	-2.9	-3.3	-3.4
Exports of goods fob (US$ bn)	79.1	101.0	115.8	126.8	132.0	140.6
Imports of goods fob (US$ bn)	70.6	83.3	96.7	109.3	119.2	131.1
Current-account balance (US$ bn)	1.6	10.2	9.0	5.6	0.7	-2.1
Current-account balance (% of GDP)	0.4	2.2	1.7	0.9	0.1	-0.3
External debt (end-period; US$ bn)	6.8	7.9	9.3	10.6	11.8	13.1
Exchange rate IR:US$ (av)	28,977	31,005	32,866	34,673	37,794	40,855
Exchange rate IR:US$ (end-period)	31,491	32,839	35,330	37,764	40,885	43,946
Exchange rate IR:¥100 (av)	23,733	24,928	26,720	28,421	31,495	34,607
Exchange rate IR:€ (end-period)	33,695	35,795	40,806	44,750	49,470	54,054

Annex B

Iran's Economic Growth (Solutions, EIU Digital 2018)

%	2015[a]	2016[b]	2017[b]	2018[b]	2019[b]	2020[b]
GDP	1.4	6.1	6.0	5.3	5.2	5.5
Private consumption	1.0	4.0	6.0	6.1	5.8	6.3
Government consumption	-1.8	3.0	5.5	5.2	5.0	5.4
Gross fixed investment	2.0	8.0	10.5	7.5	7.0	6.7
Exports of goods & services	8.0	18.0	8.0	6.1	5.5	6.0
Imports of goods & services	6.0	14.5	13.0	10.0	8.0	8.6
Domestic demand	0.6	4.6	6.6	5.9	5.6	5.9
Agriculture	0.5	2.0	2.0	1.0	1.5	1.2
Industry	2.0	7.6	5.8	5.1	4.2	4.6
Services	-0.8	1.3	6.6	5.9	6.2	6.5

Annex C

Annual Data and Forecast of Iran (Solutions, EIU Digital 2018)

	2011[a]	2012[a]	2013[a]	2014[a]	2015[b]	2016[c]	2017[c]
GDP							
Nominal GDP (US$ m)	592,038	587,209	511,621	425,326	416,188	470,422	534,668
Nominal GDP (IR trn)	6,285	7,150	9,421	11,034	12,060	14,586	17,572
Real GDP growth (%)	3.7	-6.6	-1.9	4.3	1.4	6.1	6.0
Expenditure on GDP (% real change)							
Private consumption	4.2	-1.7	-1.0	3.1	1.0	4.0	6.0
Government consumption	-3.4	-7.2	1.6	2.7	-1.8	3.0	5.5
Gross fixed investment	3.5	-23.8	-6.9	3.5	2.0	8.0	10.5
Exports of goods & services	-0.3	-20.5	0.0	12.0	8.0	18.0	8.0
Imports of goods & services	-9.4	-23.1	-18.7	-5.7	6.0	14.5	13.0
Origin of GDP (% real change)							
Agriculture	-0.1	3.7	4.7	3.8	0.5	2.0	2.0
Industry	2.6	-18.3	-4.7	4.9	2.0	7.6	5.8
Services	5.8	1.1	-1.5	2.4	-0.8	1.3	6.6
Population and income							
Population (m)	75.2	76.2	77.2[b]	78.1[b]	79.1	80.0	80.9
GDP per head (US$ at PPP)	17,949	17,275	16,710[b]	16,786[b]	17,114	18,332	19,638
Recorded unemployment (av; %)	12.3	12.2	10.4	10.3[b]	10.5	10.2	10.0
Fiscal indicators (% of GDP)							
Public-sector revenue	17.7	13.9	14.1	14.6	13.5	14.1	13.8
Public-sector expenditure	18.6	14.6	15.0	15.8	16.6	16.4	16.3
Public-sector balance	-0.8	-0.6	-0.9	-1.2	-3.1	-2.3	-2.5
Net public debt	12.9[b]	11.0[b]	10.4[b]	10.7[b]	13.1	13.4	13.9
Prices and financial indicators							
Exchange rate IR:US$ (av)	10,616	12,176	18,414	25,942	28,977	31,005	32,866
Exchange rate IR:US$ (end-period)	11,165	12,260	24,774	27,138	31,491	32,839	35,330
Consumer prices (av; %)	20.6	26.0	39.3	17.2[b]	14.7	14.0	13.6
Stock of money M1 (% change)	19.5[b]	26.7[b]	10.5[b]	7.1[b]	11.0	14.5	14.0
Stock of money M2 (% change)	20.3[b]	32.0[b]	28.1[b]	34.8[b]	17.7	26.0	25.3
Lending interest rate (av; %)	11.0	11.0	11.0	14.0	14.0	13.5	13.0
Current account (US$ m)							
Trade balance	67,779	28,559	31,969	21,392	8,471	17,645	19,098
Goods: exports fob	145,806	97,271	93,124	86,471	79,105	100,993	115,782
Goods: imports fob	-78,027	-68,712	-61,155	-65,079	-70,634	-83,348	-96,684
Services balance	-9,771	-7,306	-7,137	-6,985	-7,766	-9,510	-11,777
Income balance	93	1,661	1,066	943	381	1,594	1,231
Current transfers balance	406	510	541	511	526	505	485
Current-account balance	58,507	23,423	26,440	15,861	1,613	10,233	9,037
External debt (US$ m)							
Debt stock	15,499	7,406	7,646	6,956[b]	6,780	7,884	9,284
Debt service paid	1,649	601	405	934[b]	833	778	852
Principal repayments	1,389	446	358	683[b]	620	574	615
Interest	260	155	48	251[b]	213	204	237
International reserves (US$ m)							
Total international reserves	92,450[b]	104,650[b]	107,950[b]	108,950[b]	93,950	113,950	116,450

Annex D

Annual Trends Charts of the Iranian Economy (Solutions, EIU Digital 2018)

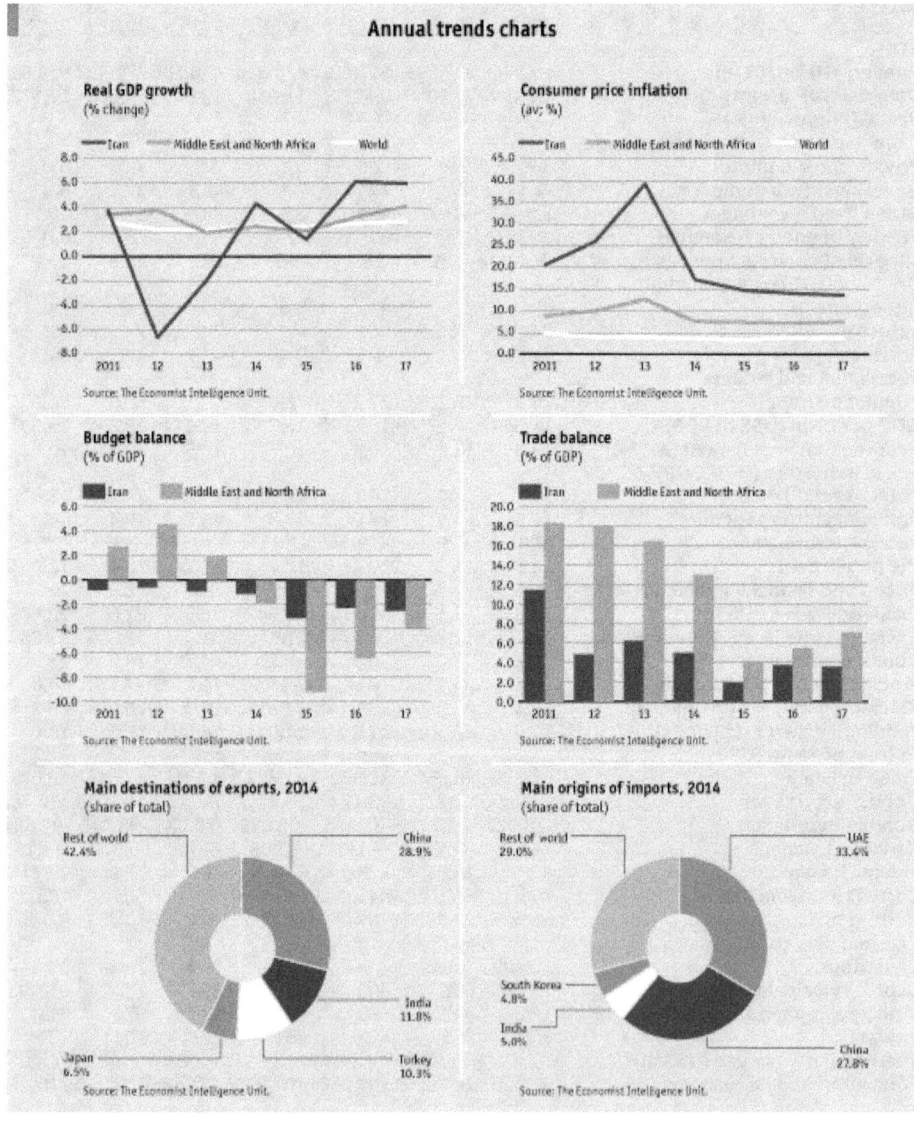

Annex E

Comparative Economic Indicators of Iran (Solutions, EIU Digital 2018)

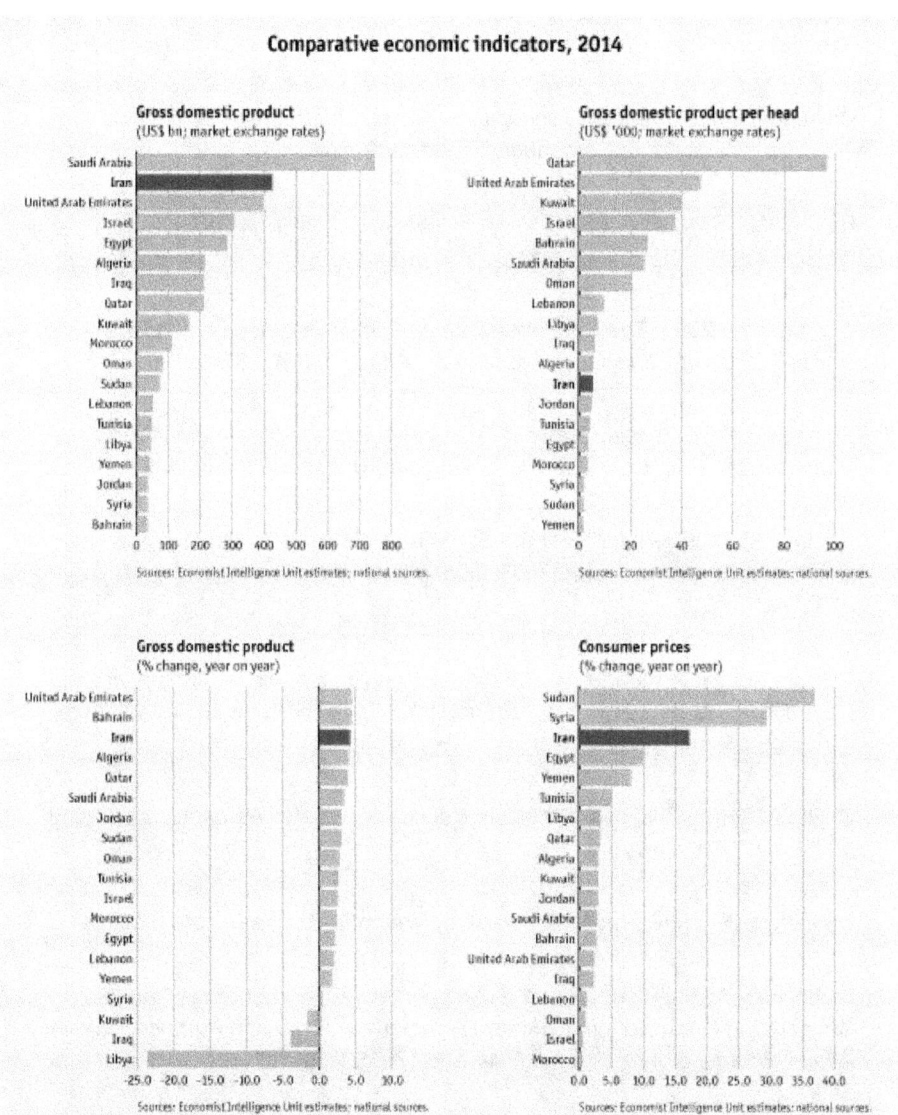

References

Allott, J. 2014. Into Syria, Out of Syria. *National Review*, 1 May 2014. https://www.nationalreview.com/magazine/2014/05/19/syria-out-syria/

Ansari, Ali M. 2007. *Confronting Iran: The Failure of American Foreign Policy and the Next Great Crisis in the Middle East*. New York: Basic Books.

Bayman, D. 2007. *Deadly Connections: States and Sponsor Terrorism*. Cambridge: Cambridge University Press.

BBC. 2018. Syria's War. *BBC News*. Accessed March 12, 2018. http://www.bbc.com/news/world-middle-east-17258397.

Brummer, M. 2007. The Shanghai Cooperation Organization and Iran: A Power-Full Union. *Journal of International Affairs*, 60(2): 185–198.

Buzan, B. 2016. *People, States & Fear: An Agenda for International Security Studies in the Post-Cold War era*. Colchester, United Kingdom: ECPR Press.

Costalli, S. 2009. "Power over the Sea: The Relevance of Neoclassical Realism to Euro-Mediterranean Relations." *Mediterranean Politics*, 14(3): 323–342.

Crowley, M., H. Mourtada, M. Calabresi, J. Newton-small, M. Thompson, K. Vick, and A. Baker. 2014. Iraq's Eternal War. *Time*, 30 June 2014. http://time.com/3326582/the-never-ending-war/

CFR. 2018. Iran's Nuclear Program. *Council on Foreign Relations*. Accessed March 12, 2018. https://www.cfr.org/backgrounder/irans-nuclear-program.

Daneshvar, P. 1996. *Revolution in Iran*. London: MacMillan Press Limited.

Dizboni, A., A. Haji-Yousefi, and G. Mcpherson. 2010. "Iran and Shanghai Cooperation Organization: Counter-Hegemony as Common Purpose." *World Affairs: Journal of International Issues*, 14(2):150-174.

Ehteshami, Anoushiravan, and Mahjoob Zweiri. 2009. *Iran and the rise of its neoconservatives: the politics of Tehrans silent revolution*. London: I.B. Tauris.

EIU Digital Solutions. 2018. *Iran Economy, Politics and GDP Growth Summary - The Economist Intelligence Unit*. Accessed March 21. http://country.eiu.com/iran.

Flems, D. 2007. Conceptualizing Regional Power in International Relations: Lessons from the South African Case. *GIGA Research Programme: Power, Violence, and Security*. No. 53, pp. 1–59.

Friedman, Dan, and Corky Siemaszko. 2018. U.S., allies destroy ISIS targets, kill terrorist leader. *NY Daily News*. September 23, 2014. Accessed March 12, 2018. http://www.nydailynews.com/news/world/photos-released-demolished-isis-buildings-u-s-airstrikes-article-1.1949839

Grammaticas, Damian. 2018. China's stake in the Syria stand-off. *BBC News*. February 24, 2012. Accessed March 12, 2018. http://www.bbc.com/news/world-asia-china-17158889.

Grubb, C. 2010. *Explaining Iran's Foreign Policy, 1979–2009*. Monterrey, CA: Naval Postgraduate School. https://calhoun.nps.edu/bitstream/handle/10945/5051/10Dec_Grubb.pdf?sequence=1&isAllowed=y

Hart, A., and B. Jones. 2011. "How do Rising Powers Rise." *Survival,* 52(6): pp. 63–88

Huntington, S. 1999. The Lonely Superpower. *Foreign Affairs*, 78(2): 35–49. https://www.foreignaffairs.com/articles/united-states/1999-03-01/lonely-superpower

Hurrell, A. 2006. Hegemony, Liberalism, and Global Order: What Space for Would-be Great Powers? *International Affairs,* 82(1): 1–19.

IMF. 2016. *Economic Implications of Agreement with the Islamic Republic of Iran*. Washington, DC: International Monetary Fund. https://www.imf.org/external/pubs/ft/reo/2015/mcd/eng/pdf/mreo1015ch5.pdf

Juneau, T. 2017. *Iranian Foreign Policy Since 2001: Alone in the World*. New York: Garland Science.

Juneau, T. 2014. Iran under Rouhani: Still Alone in the World. *Middle East Policy,* 11(4). https://onlinelibrary.wiley.com/doi/abs/10.1111/mepo.12098

Levitt, M. 2013. *Hezbollah: The Global Footprint of Lebanon's Party of God.* Washington DC: Georgetown University Press.

Limbert, J. 2009. *Negotiating with Iran.* Washington DC: United States Institute of Peace.

Ma'oz, Moshe. 2004. *Syria and Israel: From War to Peacemaking.* Oxford: Clarendon Press.

Miklos, J. 1983. *The Iranian Revolution and Modernization: Way Stations to Anarchy.* Washington DC: National Defence University Press.

Nasr, Seyyed Vali Reza. 2007. *The Shia Revival: How Conflicts within Islam will Shape the Future.* New York: W.W. Norton.

Osterud, Oyvind. 1992. Regional Great Powers. In *Regional Great Powers in International Politics,* edited by Iver B. Neumann, 1–15. New York: Springer Publishing.

Parsi, T. 2007. *Treacherous Alliance.* New Haven: Yale University Press.

Pollack, Kenneth M. 2005. *The Persian puzzle: The conflict between Iran and America.* New York: Random House.

Pti. 2015. India, Pakistan become full SCO members. *The Hindu.* July 10, 2015. Accessed March 12, 2018. http://www.thehindu.com/news/international/india-gets-full-membership-of-the-shanghai-cooperation-organisation-along-with-pakistan/article7407873.ece

Ranstorp, M. 1997. *Hizballah in Lebanon: The Politics of the Western Hostage Crisis.* New York: St. Martin's Press.

Roberts, Dan. 2018. Senate approves Obama's plan to arm and train Syrian rebels. *The Guardian.* 18 September 2014. Accessed March 12, 2018. http://www.theguardian.com/world/2014/sep/18/senate-backs-obama-syria-rebels-isis.

Ruys, T. 2014. The Syrian Civil War and the Achilles' Heel of Non-International Armed Conflict. *Stanford Journal Of International Law,* 50: 247–279.

Solutions, EIU Digital. 2018. *Iran: Annual Data and Forecast*. Accessed March 12, 2018.

http://country.eiu.com/article.aspx?articleid=453689829&Country=Iran&topic=Economy&subtopic=Charts and tables&subsubtopic=Annual data and forecast#

Solutions, EIU Digital. 2018. *Iran: Annual Trends Charts*. Accessed March 12, 2018. http://country.eiu.com/article.aspx?articleid=453689829&Country=Iran&topic=Economy&subtopic=Charts and tables&subsubtopic=Annual data and forecast#

Solutions, EIU Digital. 2018. *Iran: Comparative Economic Indicators*. Accessed March 12, 2018. http://country.eiu.com/article.aspx?articleid=603689844&Country=Iran&topic=Economy&subtopic=Charts and tables&subsubtopic=Comparative economic indicators&oid=453689829&aid=1.

Solutions, EIU Digital. 2018. *Iran: Economic Growth*. Accessed March 12, 2018. http://country.eiu.com/article.aspx?articleid=333689817&Country=Iran&topic=Economy&subtopic=Forecast&subsubtopic=Economic growth&oid=423689826&aid=1.

Solutions, EIU Digital. 2018. *Iran: Forecast Summary*. Accessed March 12, 2018. http://country.eiu.com/article.aspx?articleid=423689826&Country=Iran&topic=Economy&subtopic=Forecast&subsubtopic=Forecast summary&oid=423689826&aid=1.

Taliaferro, J. 2006. State-building for Future Wars: Neoclassical Realism and the Resource-Extractive State. *Security Studies,* 15(3): 464–495.

Tank, P. 2013. The Concept of 'Rising Powers.' *Noref Policy Brief*. https://www.files.ethz.ch/isn/146521/aa7c23bf5887ab060f1af737a39a000a.pdf

Tayekh, R. 2005. Iran Builds the Bomb. *Survival,* 46(4): 51–63.

Vakil, S. 2006. Iran: Balancing East against West. *The Washington Quarterly,* 29(4): 51–65.

Walsh, L. 2018. *Final Report of the Independent Counsel for Iran/Contra Matters*. Walsh Iran / Contra Report - Part I Iran/contra: The Underlying Facts. Accessed March 12, 2018. http://www.fas.org/irp/offdocs/walsh/part_i.htm.

Watson, M. 2001. *Balance of Power vs Balance of Threat: The Case of China and Pakistan.* Quantico: Marine Corps University Press.

Wohlfort, W. 1991. The Stability of a Unipolar World. *International Security,* 24(1): 5–41.

Note on Indexing

E-IR's publications do not feature indexes. If you are reading this book in paperback and want to find a particular word or phrase you can do so by downloading a free PDF version of this book from the E-International Relations website.

View the e-book in any standard PDF reader such as Adobe Acrobat Reader (pc) or Preview (mac) and enter your search terms in the search box. You can then navigate through the search results and find what you are looking for. In practice, this method can prove much more targeted and effective than consulting an index.

If you are using apps (or devices) to read our e-books, you should also find word search functionality in those.

You can find all of our e-books at: http://www.e-ir.info/publications

www.ingramcontent.com/pod-product-compliance
Lightning Source LLC
Chambersburg PA
CBHW071453080526
44587CB00014B/2091